# A
# BLESSING
# IN
# DISGUISE

# ALSO BY IMMACULÉE ILIBAGIZA

*THE BOY WHO MET JESUS: Segatashya of Kibeho*

*LED BY FAITH: Rising from the Ashes of the Rwandan
Genocide* (also available as an abridged audio book)

*LEFT TO TELL: Discovering God Amidst the Rwandan
Holocaust* (also available in Spanish and as
an abridged audio book)

*OUR LADY OF KIBEHO: Mary Speaks to the World
from the Heart of Africa* (also available in Spanish)

*THE ROSARY: The Prayer that Saved My Life*


All of the above are available at your local bookstore,
or may be ordered by visiting:

Hay House UK: www.hayhouse.co.uk
Hay House USA: www.hayhouse.com®
Hay House Australia: www.hayhouse.com.au
Hay House India: www.hayhouse.co.in

\*\*\*

# A BLESSING IN DISGUISE

Miracles *of the*
Seven Sorrows Rosary

IMMACULÉE ILIBAGIZA

**HAY HOUSE**

Carlsbad, California • New York City
London • Sydney • New Delhi

**Published in the United Kingdom by:**
Hay House UK Ltd, The Sixth Floor, Watson House,
54 Baker Street, London W1U 7BU
Tel: +44 (0)20 3927 7290; Fax: +44 (0)20 3927 7291; www.hayhouse.co.uk

**Published in the United States of America by:**
Hay House Inc., PO Box 5100, Carlsbad, CA 92018-5100
Tel: (1) 760 431 7695 or (800) 654 5126
Fax: (1) 760 431 6948 or (800) 650 5115; www.hayhouse.com

**Published in Australia by:**
Hay House Australia Ltd, 18/36 Ralph St, Alexandria NSW 2015
Tel: (61) 2 9669 4299; Fax: (61) 2 9669 4144; www.hayhouse.com.au

**Published in India by:**
Hay House Publishers India, Muskaan Complex, Plot No.3, B-2,
Vasant Kunj, New Delhi 110 070
Tel: (91) 11 4176 1620; Fax: (91) 11 4176 1630; www.hayhouse.co.in

*Cover design:* Amy Grigoriou
*Interior design:* Karim J. García
*Illustration of Mother Mary on p.50:* Jami Goddess

A catalogue record for this book is available from the British Library.

Tradepaper ISBN: 978-1-78817-187-8
E-book ISBN: 978-1-4019-5031-6
Audiobook ISBN: 978-1-4019-5865-7

Printed in Great Britain by CPI (UK) Ltd, Croydon CR0 4YY

"To the Virgin Mary, the sweetest, most loving, and most merciful Mother, praying your chapels in Kibeho will be built as you wanted them and where you wanted. I promise to continue to do my best to spread the Seven Sorrows Rosary. Mother, help me. To Marie-Claire, the messenger of Mary, thank you for passing on the torch, for your good work, and for your sacrifice. Pray for me."

# CONTENTS

# INTRODUCTION

## *The Gift of the Seven Sorrows*

It has been almost 40 years, but I will never forget the first time I heard about the Seven Sorrows Rosary. One of my neighbors, who had just come from Kibeho, Rwanda, was the one who told me about it.

I was already familiar with the southern Rwandan village of Kibeho. In 1981, it was the magnificent site of a series of apparitions of the Virgin Mary, as well as her son, Jesus. At that time, as incredible as it sounds, the Virgin Mary and Jesus began appearing to a group of young people in Kibeho. The visionaries were given messages from heaven intended for the entire world to hear: messages of love, faith, how to come closer to God, how to pray more effectively, and how to love one another. She informed the visionaries that if the world did not change their ways, we would not have peace, and we would fall into ruin.

It was 17-year-old Alphonsine Mumureke (who was serving food to her fellow students in the dining room of Kibeho High School, a Catholic boarding school run by the Benebikira Sisters) to whom the Mother of God first appeared—identifying herself as "the Mother of the Word." However, it was the initially skeptical 21-year-old student, Marie-Claire Mukangango, to whom the

Blessed Virgin revealed the sacred Seven Sorrows Rosary, a prayer that leads her followers through the Seven Sorrows of Mary's life.

The woman from whom I first learned about the Seven Sorrows Rosary came to the chapel in my village, which my father had built so that the villagers would have a place where they could gather to pray the traditional rosary. She was effusive about the miracles that were taking place in Kibeho. When I saw her, she was talking to a few people who were outside the chapel. Her face was radiating with an intense internal joy, but sometimes also pain. I could tell that something major had happened to her. It was almost as if her feet weren't touching the ground. I approached so that I could hear her better. I was 12 years old, and she was 18 at the time; in my mind, she was very old, so I didn't dare ask much, as the adults were having a conversation. However, I listened intently, afraid to miss a single word of her remarkable story.

The young woman was discussing the Seven Sorrows Rosary, which Mary had taught the visionary Marie-Claire and was now sharing with anyone who paid a pilgrimage to this holy site. This prayer was completely new to me. The people in my village always met to say the traditional rosary, but not this one.

"We walked on foot for three days to get to Kibeho," she shared. "We slept on the ground for one night once we got there, and then we turned around and walked back for three more days. We were all very tired, and some people got sick, while others had blisters on their feet. But we were all safe the whole time. During our pilgrimage, Mary was with us and showed us signs of her presence. At one point, somebody got sick and we all prayed over her, invoking Mary's help for our friend, who healed right in front of our eyes! On another night, we saw an unusual star that seemed to be shining very close to us and guiding us."

As the woman went on to explain the components of the Seven Sorrows Rosary—a prayer that depicts and encompasses the pain that Mary endured through the life of her son, Our Lord Jesus Christ—I felt my own world touched and transformed.

Immediately, I knew that I needed to learn this prayer.

Soon after, we all went into the small chapel to pray. It was a heavenly spot that sat atop a hill that was not the tallest in our village but allowed everyone a view of the surrounding mountains. On one side of the chapel, one could see the main church in the town of Mushubati; on another side was the flowing Muregeya River; and then, on another side, Lake Kivu and the green hills of Congo. Inside the chapel, my father asked the young woman to lead us in the Seven Sorrows Rosary. She led us through each of the sorrows, which surprised me, as she had so quickly memorized the meditations and spoke with the authority of her emotions. We all then went outside quietly and returned home in deep thought. The experience had been a strange one in that I felt both uplifted by the sublime beauty of the prayer but also struck by the depth of Mary's sorrow, which felt very human. It was almost as if Mary's pain had become our own—but unexpectedly, my own sufferings had disappeared. I had felt Our Mother's sorrow so deeply, but my own heart was so light. Although I'd shed a few tears during the prayer, I felt renewed, as if praying on Mary's Sorrows were a blessing in disguise.

As a young girl, I had always been a devout lover of Mary and Jesus. I was named after the Virgin Mary, as my name, Immaculée, honors her Immaculate Conception. Even my surname, Ilibagiza, is a name given to Mary in my native language, Kinyarwanda. It translates to "She was beautiful in body and soul." Because my father had lost his own mother, he found a mother in Mary. I grew up with such pride that I'd been named after the Mother of God.

When I was in fourth grade, during catechism class, my schoolteacher read to me and my classmates about the miracle that took place in 1917 when the Blessed Virgin appeared to three young peasant children in Fátima, Portugal, with a message of peace and hope. I dreamt of receiving similar apparitions. In my childish mind, I believed that if I did as the children of Fátima did—becoming a shepherd and reciting the rosary—I, too, would have apparitions! I convinced two friends, a boy and a girl, to join me; and every evening, we followed my parents' cows and said the rosary so that Mary would come to us. A month passed, and although we never saw Mary, she began to appear in Kibeho.

My heartfelt joy at the possibility of directly receiving her messages never left my heart, so I quickly became invested in the goings-on at Kibeho, which would last for more than a decade (and even today, the remaining visionaries are still blessed with apparitions). Several other young people in Kibeho, aside from the three girls who became the central figures in the miracle, would claim to have apparitions of Mary and Jesus. It was a period that utterly changed my life, as well as the lives of many people in my country, and I would grow up to become friends with some of the visionaries from Kibeho and to help make some of the wishes Our Lady revealed to them a reality.

Before I learned the Seven Sorrows Rosary, the love I'd felt for Mary had always felt similar to the love one feels for a distant star; that is, all I could think about was how beautiful, holy, and perfect she seemed. She was special, and no human could take the place I had for her in my heart. The visionaries described her as the most beautiful woman they'd ever seen. They said she resembled a young bride dressed in white, sometimes with a mantle an unusual shade of bright blue. She stood in a field of flowers and was surrounded by a very soft but very bright light. She exuded a motherly love that was so pure it was difficult to put into words.

All these descriptions provoked my deepest yearnings for connection with her. And when I encountered the Seven Sorrows Rosary, I recognized something deeper; Mary was suddenly much closer at hand, occupying space in the back of my heart. Far be it from a distant holy being, she was right here with me, and I with her.

The Seven Sorrows Rosary, which focuses on seven events of Mary's life during which she became an intimate witness to the sacrifice of her son, has the unique power to open a person's heart to the depth of their own sorrow. When I was a young girl, the prayer reverberated within my soul. In contemplating Mary's sorrows, I encountered flashbacks to every sorrow I'd felt in my young life—from fearing for my mother due to her asthma, to almost losing my father when he became severely ill after an allergic reaction to penicillin. In contemplating my pain this way, I drew closer to Mary's suffering and felt her in a way that I never had before. I saw her as my friend, and I learned from her how to suffer without complaining, making sinful decisions, or holding grudges that would continue to hurt me. It was almost as if she were standing over me, asking, "Do you want me to be part of you in this way, my child? Will you open your heart to me and share your pain with me? Will you let me bring God's healing into your life?"

## THE LIGHT AT THE END OF THE HORROR

Unfortunately, along with the messages of peace, love, repentance, faith, and renewal that Our Lady of Kibeho brought, she also gave us many warnings that hatred, division, and sin would lead Rwanda and the rest of the world into a dark abyss of bloodshed and death if we did not change. Today, it is the Virgin Mary's prophecy of the 1994 genocide in Rwanda that has caused hundreds of thousands to remember the apparitions in Kibeho.

I am a survivor of that genocide, which devastated my beautiful homeland of Rwanda. I was a 24-year-old university student when a government-backed holocaust of unimaginable evil was unleashed upon my country's minority tribe, the Tutsis. To be Tutsi in Rwanda, like my family, was a death sentence. In less than 100 days, almost the entire Tutsi population of Rwanda—more than a million innocent men, women, and children—were mercilessly tortured, raped, and butchered during what is now acknowledged as one of the most vicious campaigns of ethnic cleansing in human history. Almost every member of my immediate and extended family was murdered during the slaughter, and so was just about every other person I had ever loved or called a friend.

I survived, thanks to the kindness of a local pastor who took mercy on me and seven other Tutsi women by hiding us in a tiny bathroom for three months. This was a journey I explored in my book *The Rosary: The Prayer That Saved My Life*. In it, I share the fear and despair that were my constant companions and worst enemies as killers hunted me. Thoughts of opening the door and ending the torture of waiting for the killers to find me plagued me, and the devil whispered in my ear. But even during the darkest days of my life, I was able to find God and fill my heart with a love that enabled me to forgive those who had killed my family. This led me to become an international teacher spreading the message of love, hope, and our human potential for forgiveness and rebuilding a world of love according to God's ways. Over the last decades, I have shared what I know to be true with world leaders, schoolchildren, churches, and hundreds of thousands of souls longing for release from suffering across the globe.

My experiences during the genocide and its aftermath are chronicled in my first two books, *Left to Tell: Discovering God Amidst the Rwandan Holocaust* and *Led by Faith: Rising from the Ashes of the Rwandan Genocide*. If you are interested in how faith and forgiveness became my guiding lights in a world darkened by hatred and despair, please read them both.

Of course, like everyone, my life is not perfect. I still go through pain and setbacks. I have experienced heartache, insecurity, doubt, and betrayal. However, I draw comfort from understanding that praying will always bring me closer to God. The closer I am to him, the more his love will sustain and uplift me, no matter how my life looks or how hopeless things may seem.

Although, over the years, I didn't say the Seven Sorrows Rosary every day, as I did the traditional rosary, it always remained in my heart, and I continued to come back to it. There is something about the presence of the Virgin Mary that does not disappear from a person's life once it has touched them so deeply. In her, we recognize the presence of our mother, the one who comforts us with her gentle reassurances and the supernatural capacity to sit with us through our suffering.

In Kibeho, Our Lady said, "Pray the rosary not as Catholics, but as my children, and you will experience my help and heavenly peace in your lives." Anyone can pray with the traditional rosary,[1] as well as the Seven Sorrows Rosary, which Our Lady offered for the benefit of all her children. It is a most remarkable prayer, as it can be offered for any strife one might be experiencing—nothing is too big or small. We can pray on our own behalf, or for the benefit of loved ones, entire communities, and even the world. I know from the spiritual work I have done with the Seven Sorrows Rosary over many decades that it has the power to change us from the inside out. As we pray with Mary through the Seven Sorrows she experienced, our hearts break open with empathy, not just for her suffering and the suffering of Our Lord but also for the suffering we experience on a daily basis, sometimes without even recognizing it.

The Seven Sorrows Rosary deepens our awareness of our suffering, as well as the sins that may have led us to turn away from the miracles of love that God has offered to us as our birthright. Judeo-Christian theology reminds us that one definition of sin is missing the mark of the moral standards that God has set for humanity. God gave us his commandments and guidance for how to live a good life that will bring us joy and peace.

Essentially, when we sin, we fall short of God's glory and we hurt ourselves in the long run. We seldom realize that in doing so, we perpetuate our own and others' suffering, as our sin takes us further and further away from God's protection—and further and further away from our true selves. We were created by love, to love

---

[1] The Catholic rosary is the summary of the Bible, a set of prayers that are arranged in sets of 10 Hail Marys, called decades. Each decade is preceded by one Lord's Prayer (Our Father) followed by one Glory Be. Each rosary includes five mysteries, which recall events in the lives of Jesus and Mary. The rosary beads are meant to aid us in saying these prayers in the proper sequence. Pope Pius V (1566–1572) established 15 mysteries of the rosary, which encompass three sets of the Joyful, Sorrowful, and Glorious Mysteries. In 2002, Pope John Paul II added a new set of five mysteries known as the Luminous Mysteries. It is customary for Catholics to pray the rosary daily; the Glorious Mysteries on Sunday and Wednesday; the Joyful on Monday and Saturday; the Sorrowful on Tuesday and Friday; and the Luminous on Thursday. However, in Kibeho and Fátima, the Virgin Mary asked that we pray the entire rosary every day, then the 15 mysteries (Joyful, Sorrowful, and Glorious). If we can't pray the whole rosary, Our Mother suggested that we pray at least one. Mary gave 15 promises for those who say the rosary from the heart; among them, she promised to grant us anything we ask for, through the prayer of the rosary.

and be loved. We dishonor his intentions for us, as we were made in his image and can truly find peace and contentment only by abiding in his ways. As St. Augustine said, "Our hearts are restless until they rest in God."

In walking the same path as the Blessed Virgin Mary, a completely sinless woman who witnessed the unspeakable suffering of her son, Jesus Christ, with absolute love and without a sinful or vengeful thought or feeling, we transform our pain into freedom. We allow ourselves to express the depth of our sorrow, and to surrender it to the Blessed Virgin. All of this helps us to live a life that is free from denial, repression, and bitterness. We learn to walk in the path of Our Lady and Our Lord so that we can experience greater clarity, courage, and joy—and so we can accept, understand, and be a meaningful part of the world around us.

The Virgin Mary recommended that we pray the Seven Sorrows Rosary daily, but especially in times of need. We pray the Seven Sorrows Rosary whenever we require the guidance and love of the Blessed Virgin, and when we need to be reminded that our suffering, even when it seems endless, will not go on forever. In fact, it is our capacity to endure sorrow that deepens our capacity for love, tenderness, compassion, and joy.

## THE CALL TO WRITE A BOOK ABOUT THE SEVEN SORROWS ROSARY

Rwanda is a nation with a strong oral culture; stories, prayers, and teachings are passed down orally, and when I was growing up, very few people in my village had books they could refer to. Thus, if our hearts were touched by a prayer, we memorized it rather than referring to a piece of writing in a pamphlet or book.

By the time I found myself living in the United States permanently, I had a strong desire to share everything I have learned about the Seven Sorrows Rosary with others, but I hadn't memorized it, which I felt was necessary in order to teach it to others.

This would soon change. One night, I had a dream that somebody, perhaps an angel or Mary herself, was making me open my mouth to repeat the words in the Seven Sorrows Rosary, so that I memorized them. Soon, the prayers were effortlessly flowing from my tongue! When I awoke, I was still repeating the prayers. I was dumbfounded. I had completed the rosary in the dream, and now I was able to recite it without using a booklet for reference. I finally felt I had the divine knowledge to teach it to others. When I gave my next retreat, I started to teach it and actually pray it with other people. This was and still is the most loved session of my retreats. People constantly share what a relief it is to step into this beautiful prayer.

In a twist of fate, a woman in Kibeho who was devoted to the Virgin Mary suggested that on top of teaching the Seven Sorrows Rosary, I write a book about it. I inquired, "What would you want to see me write about?" She replied, "Anything—whatever is in your heart, including your perspectives and understanding of the rosary."

I kept this suggestion in mind, but because I had many other projects to work on, I knew it might take me some years before I could return to it. But the subject arose again when I was facilitating a retreat in the U.S. I asked the assembled crowd if anyone had any questions, and one woman responded: "When are you going to write a book on the Seven Sorrows Rosary?" I asked her what she'd like me to write about, and she responded, "A book that covers anything you want to share about the rosary, including your perspective on its power and the miracles associated with it."

I was shocked to hear almost the same words as I had from the woman in Kibeho. I had previously written a booklet on the subject of how to pray the Seven Sorrows Rosary, and I'd also believed that referencing it during my travels—on pilgrimages and at retreats—was enough. But clearly this was not so.

I went home with a smile in my heart. I knew it was time to share my love for the Seven Sorrows Rosary and all my thoughts about this beautiful prayer that is already a blessing to so many. I realized that although I had been doing my best to put the book idea on the back burner and focus on other goals, Our Lady was clearly sending me a message to pay attention to the spiritual power of the Seven Sorrows. It seemed to me that it was the perfect time—a time filled with deep suffering across the globe. Thus, the book was brought once more to the forefront of my heart.

That same night, when I woke up, the earth was still quiet—my favorite time of the day. I couldn't sleep, so I started to think about Our Lady and all she had suffered. I spent more than an hour feeling like I had left where I was; suddenly, I was in Israel and in Egypt with Mary, and then I was in Jerusalem, looking for Jesus when he was lost. Soon, I was a friend of Mary, helping her walk beside her son on the way to the cross. I was there watching her tears as she stood beneath the cross. My heart broke when she received his lifeless body in her arms. Then I was at his tomb when she lost her final ounce of strength. Tears were pouring down my cheeks.

For a moment, I had to forget that she is the Mother of God and the Queen of Heaven, which can be intimidating to ponder or can make one believe that she had superpowers that made it easier for her to bear the intense suffering of her son. But I was able to connect to the very human part of Mary—the part that watched her beautiful son become the object of brutal hatred and ridicule. This pure lady was given a mission to be the Mother of Jesus, the Son of God—surely it is the best blessing that has ever existed. She had to have also undergone some rare, precious, and sacred experiences in the time that her son was alive—but in losing him to the cruelty of his captors and executioners, she was subjected to the kind of agony that no mother should ever have to face. Her love came with a price, which she paid to God by giving his only son as a sacrifice for the world's sins.

The more I thought about all she endured, the more I recognized Mary as an intrinsic part of our salvation.

As I ruminated on her sorrows, I began to think of my own suffering. I thought of the pain that I had experienced throughout my life, but my thoughts traveled far beyond the personal. I began to consider all the pain that so many of us bury so deeply that we never give ourselves a chance to feel it. I also started thinking about all the pain and wickedness that cause many of us the world over to suffer, without reprieve. I was engulfed with a deep spiritual sorrow that seemed to take me into the heart of the human condition. The quality of this pain was sharp, searing, bitter . . . but not once did I feel alone inside this suffering. I felt as if standing over me was Our Lady, who had already gone through the worst travails, and who is now in heaven. I felt her presence, almost like a healing balm soothing my wounds, whispering sweet words of mercy and compassion as I wept.

After this extraordinary experience, after all the tears had been wept, I was at peace. I spoke to her of my pain and how it hurt, and how unfair it was. I knew that she understood me perfectly. In speaking with her, I was removing the pain from the insular shelter of my heart and to the outside, where it could be cleansed. If somebody spoke to me unkindly, I told her about it. She knew what it is to be rejected, to be hated, to be hurt. I felt that in meditating on her suffering, I was growing in my capacity to love my enemies. I was growing in my capacity to look at my individual moments of suffering not as a terrible, frightful ordeal, but as periods that enabled me to unite myself with Jesus and Mary, and learn from them. I felt such a desire to tell everyone about this miraculous prayer, which has the power to open different doors of the heart and heal the fractured self. I wanted everyone to know the grace and joy that would follow them in contemplating Mary's Seven Sorrows, and offering their prayers to one who had withstood the agony of her son's death without falling into hopelessness, despair, or thoughts of revenge.

At last, the seed was planted. I knew that I would do my best to create a book that would contain powerful storytelling about the miracles of the Seven Sorrows Rosary, which I have seen firsthand in both my life and the lives of people I've encountered across the world, as well as a comprehensive manual for anyone interested in the powerful spiritual practice that Our Mother so graciously offered when she revealed the Seven Sorrows to St. Bridget of Sweden—and once more, many centuries later, to Marie-Claire of Kibeho, Rwanda. I've heard countless testimonials about how the Seven Sorrows have transformed lives shattered by depression and despair, offered hope and miracles to people estranged from loved ones, answered the prayers of women who longed to become pregnant but who faced severe fertility issues, cured addiction and disease, and filled lonely hearts with joy and purpose. I have seen how the Seven Sorrows have worked wonders in the lives of people everywhere, including the most devout Catholics and those without any religious affiliation whatsoever.

Please know that the Seven Sorrows is for all people, all of whom Our Mother considers her children. To that end, even if you are not familiar with the Catholic rituals and scripture that are interspersed throughout this book, *A Blessing in Disguise* is for everyone who knows that even the smallest prayers can be answered with a little faith. The entirety of the Rosary ritual is included in Chapter 3.

## THE POWER OF PRAYER

No one who practices religion can argue against the importance of prayer, and even those who don't necessarily call it prayer have recognized the power of meditation to lift us out of our suffering and offer us hope and peace. We intuitively understand the value of simply being with ourselves as we are; in allowing our hearts and minds a quiet space where we can listen to the voice within; in surrendering ourselves to God and releasing the burdens that may be weighing on us.

Mother Teresa said it well—when it comes to prayer, "More prayer, more power, less prayer, less power, no prayer, no power." St. John Vianney also noted the beauty and power of prayer in returning to our true self and joy as children of a loving God: "Prayer is the inner bath of love into which the soul plunges itself."

This is why we pray. This is why people, knowingly or not, take time to be alone—because our very nature is such that we can't find peace until we find it in silence, until we let God speak to us and we speak back to him.

An important aspect of prayer is that we release the need to show up as perfect beings. We show up as we are, with all our sins and imperfections, and we offer ourselves up to Our Lord's mercy. I once heard a therapist say that during a session, it is of the utmost importance that a patient remembers their pain and their errors, and to feel safe enough to admit to them. Otherwise, there can be no healing. It does us no good to close our eyes to the presence of our own suffering, to say, "It's okay, I'm fine," even as we are hurting inside. Many people don't have space in their lives to admit that they are in deep pain, either to themselves or to a therapist or loved one. I have met people who work hard and are very successful—at least within worldly paradigms of success. They expand their businesses and make a lot of money, which is not inherently bad, but some of them don't take the time to pray; thus, they feel little to no peace within themselves. They seek out joy by setting and fulfilling another goal, only to reach it and realize they still feel empty inside. They don't stop to consider what their souls need to heal. They don't realize that they have numbed themselves to the full spectrum of their feelings.

But it is so necessary to be real about what we are feeling, especially in the world today, if we wish to experience the sweet relief of knowing we are never alone. Even if we can't do this with a trusted human confidant, we can be assured that the Blessed Virgin and Our Lord are always close at hand—and that entrusting our hearts and cares to them can lead to the most beautiful transformations of all.

This is how I see prayer of the Seven Sorrows Rosary: it is similar to being in the presence of the wisest and most compassionate therapist and feeling free to confess what's really happening for me beneath the surface of my conscious thoughts and everyday behavior, as if someone is helping me to unburden my heart through confession, all the while reminding me that God and the Virgin Mary are always watching over me with a loving, patient gaze.

Prayer can be as simple as offering words of love or gratitude, but there is a lot of power in sharing the totality of what we are feeling, even the most difficult parts (which can be hard to admit to ourselves, let alone others), which is possible through sharing Mary's pain in the Seven Sorrows Rosary. When we share our pain with one who understands, we feel an enormous sense of relief. That night when I prayed the Seven Sorrows, I experienced a relief like nothing I had ever felt before. I was deeply consoled, and I could feel my heart opening even wider. I had prayed the Seven Sorrows many times before, but never like this—in a state of profound meditation and heartfelt empathy for everything Our Mother endured.

Mary and Jesus suffered for me, for us. You can think about this and know it on an intellectual level, but it requires a certain depth and engagement with her story in order to *feel* it, and to understand what her story has to do with you. What I understood that night is that Jesus and Mary suffered more than most humans because they loved so perfectly. They suffered not only in terms of the mental and physical afflictions they faced but also in terms of enduring this torment at the hands of people toward whom they only ever felt love—even in Jesus's final anguished hours.

Jesus said in dying, "Forgive them, Father, for they know not what they do." This pronouncement was a prayer that came from a place of love. Think of a mother who is being hurt by her children. As sorrowful as she may feel, she is incapable of hating them—and yet she still feels the pangs of disappointment in the choices they made, which create suffering all around. With deep love, we open ourselves to the reality of suffering, for this is what it means to be human.

That recognition took me to a new place in my devotion. I felt even closer to my Heavenly Mother. I felt deeply loved and cherished after the tears I wept in her company. When we feel this kind of love, we naturally long for others to experience the same thing. Likewise, if we are hurting inside but have no outlet to express it we are more likely to want to spread that hurt to others, even if we are only doing so unconsciously. Sadly, those who carry hatred, anger, and unkindness in their hearts numb themselves from fully feeling and experiencing emotional pain—which, in truth, is a gift because it helps us to grow our compassion for others who suffer. Love and empathy go hand in hand. As St. Augustine is quoted as saying, "Those who are healthy emotionally and mentally can feel everything, joy and pain." And even though it may seem counterintuitive, those who are capable of welcoming and fully experiencing pain have a greater capacity for love and joy. We see this in the sacred stories of Mary and Jesus, who offer us an example of the beautiful ways in which our suffering can transform us when we turn to it with open hearts. Jesus is King of Heaven, and nothing was reduced of him when he suffered. Mary is the Queen of Heaven and Earth—yes, she suffered, but she earned a great reward because she suffered well. With this book, I hope that you, dear reader, will see that suffering well bears its own fruits.

## THE POWER OF OUR MOTHER

For centuries, the Blessed Virgin has been a steward for the disconsolate and powerless; she has urged us to come home to our true selves and to God. Her message of unconditional love is especially comforting in this time of pervasive darkness and suffering, as we experience the uncertainty of a global pandemic, a war in Ukraine, as well as great political, economic, and environmental instability.

We can see Mary as an image of Christianity, in that she exemplifies all the exalted characteristics of woman. She has the qualities of mercy, forgiveness, compassion, tenderness, softness, gentleness, and maternal love—but also the purity, righteousness, and strength that have the power to cross evil. Even though most Mary statues represent a humble and sweet woman, she is also standing on the snake and crushing it. As the Holy Mother, she experienced a direct relationship to God on behalf of us all. Mary's qualities, far from turning us into hermits on a

mountaintop, encourage us to engage more intimately with everything in our lives so that it can be transmuted by God and so
that we can return to him. Mary is also a reminder of the value
of surrendering to God. In letting go of her identity as the earthly
mother of Christ, she became a spiritual mother to all. Her life is a
vivid lesson for what it means to let go of our selfish desires for our
loved ones and to trust wholly in God, as we all ultimately belong
to God and must answer to him.

On that special night, as I was thinking about Mary and
everything she lived through, I couldn't help but remember my
deceased mother. Every time I think about her love for me, I think
of the times she suffered for me, the times she was scared for me;
for those are the times when I could palpably feel her love. Certainly I have memories of the times when she bought me new
clothing or cooked a delicious meal for me. All of this makes me
happy, but these moments alone don't convince me of my mother's deep love.

Once, when I was about eight years old, I decided to make
some tea in our traditional kitchen, which was made up of three
stones that were not quite stable. I was in third grade at the time,
so I arrived home earlier than my mother. We also had a person
who helped us with household chores, who was also not yet home.
I found a pot of boiling water in the kitchen, which I attempted
to remove with my hands and one small tissue offering a buffer
between the scalding pot and my skin. Unfortunately, the entire
contents of the pot spilled out and onto the fire. Instead of the
water putting out the fire, I was horrified when a combination of
rising flames and scalding water vapor rose up from the ground
and came close to my face and arms. In a panic, I rubbed myself,
only to have an entire layer of skin peel off my arm, from my
fingers to my elbow. As I gazed at my red, blistered skin, I was in
a daze of pain, panic, and confusion. Just then, my mother came
back. I will never forget the distress in her eyes as she saw what
had happened to me. She immediately attended to me, but she
was also furious as she called the adults who were supposed to

be home and demanded to know why no one had been there to look after me.

In my eyes, my mother was a superwoman. Where I had been stricken by terror just moments before, her love was the curative. Once she arrived, I knew I didn't need to worry about anything else, as I was back in her arms where I belonged. Whatever she judged right was it. Nobody else in my life, not even my father, had the power to comfort me and assuage my pain. I knew that my mother instinctively understood what needed to be done.

But who was there when Mom was sick? Instead of asking for help, she tried to hide her pain from us, even if it was obvious, to protect us from worrying. My mom had asthma all her life, and when she suffered from an asthma attack, she simply closed the door to her room. I remember remaining on my knees as long as she was still coughing, holding my breath with her and begging God to save her life.

When I think of this, it makes me think of Mary. There is so much of her pain we don't know—only the pain that she shared with us, for her goal was not to share all of her suffering, only the aspects of her suffering that would be redemptive for us . . . that is, the suffering she felt with respect to her son—the way, the truth, and the life. In doing so, she leads us not to her as a final destination but to the ultimate itself: to life, to love, to Jesus.

As I thought about Mary's sufferings and her journey with Jesus, a part of me felt terribly bad for her, but similar to my own experience with my mother, a part of me also felt reassured that I have a Heavenly Mother who truly loves me, who understands pain, who loved Our Lord so much that he found deep solace in her. When I cry over her sorrows, an indissoluble bond is forged between her and me.

I have since seen this bond replicated among those who have had the courage to draw close to Mary's suffering and to observe the Seven Sorrows with open hearts. I have witnessed miracles in the realm of love, money, health, and renewed possibility. This is the great power of Our Mother. We turn to her in times of personal crisis, and like a beloved maternal figure she always hears us when we call.

So many people in our world have fallen prey to physical, psychological, economic, and spiritual hardship that can feel overwhelming to many of us. But in these times, Our Mother remains a steadfast source of comfort and hope. She offers us the kind of healing that only a mother truly can.

## THE CROSS WE BEAR

Not long ago, somebody gave me a special prayer request. I was going to Kibeho to pray, and this person told me, "Tell Mary and Jesus that I don't like the idea of suffering. If they love me, tell them to protect me from it."

I don't like suffering either, but it is a part of life that we must learn to accept. We must also acknowledge that everyone endures suffering at some point in their lives. Truly, the best way to avoid it is to learn how to deal with it—and one important way to do this is through acceptance.

I learned the power of acceptance as a child in Rwanda. I began planting pumpkin seeds in the yard where I played. In Rwanda, we don't decorate pumpkins; rather, we use them in our cooking. My family was overjoyed that my pumpkins quickly shot up from the ground and flourished. Soon enough, we had so many pumpkins that my mother would give them away to neighbors for free. In my country, we believe that certain people have a natural green thumb and anything they plant will grow. Well, that role was bestowed upon me, much to my reluctance. Suddenly everyone wanted me to plant pumpkins for them. Every day, my parents would wake me up at 3 in the morning to plant pumpkin seeds, since it was believed that in order for the seeds to take root they had to be placed in the ground very early in the day. As a child, I hated this routine, but on another level I also enjoyed it. I loved the process of patiently waiting for the seed to grow into a pumpkin so that I could then share this bounty with others. I also loved the joy my efforts brought so many people, who showed their gratitude by bringing my family and me treats made from the pumpkins I'd grown. I accepted my responsibility wholeheartedly, even if it was difficult at times.

It is the same with the work I do today. Since writing my first book, *Left to Tell*, I get invited to speak in different parts of the world to share my story and the lessons I learned during the genocide in Rwanda. I talk about forgiveness and hope, and I also share my discovery of God's love during that time. I love speaking to people around the world about my life and what it means to place our trust and faith in a God who will never fail us—whose love provides a glorious example that helps us to walk the path of hope, forgiveness, and everlasting renewal. At the same time, I don't particularly like the hassles of traveling—from getting on a plane, to dealing with the logistics of being in a new place, to experiencing constant jet lag and disorientation because I am always on the go. But still, just as when I was a child, it is the planting of the seeds of divine love that outweighs any difficulties I might experience. There is no other work for me; I was created for this—for the purpose of inspiring people and offering them the tools to emerge from depression and hopelessness and to feel better. God has his own unique ways of calling each of us, and with every blessing comes a cross to bear. But when we accept that cross with grace and humility, even that can be beautiful.

I hope that as you read this book, you will recognize the invitation that Mary has for you—to love your unique cross. For without the labor we exert, we cannot enjoy its fruits. This doesn't mean we have to plaster a smile on our faces and pretend that it doesn't hurt; in fact, the more we share our pain with Our Mother, the greater the opportunity to see it transformed into joy within the vessel of God's love.

Mary is a stunning example of what it means to never let our suffering turn us against goodness. In fact, when we are hurt by others, the best thing we can do is pray for them. Those who do evil require the most dramatic change of heart—and with prayer, all things are possible. When we pray for our enemies, we rob them of the power to do evil. We are asking God to give them the graces they need to open their eyes to see the evil they do—and to have the strength to stop it. When someone displays a weakness and we don't like their ways, it is time to offer them love, not to curse them. We can certainly share our sorrows with Our Lady, but we ourselves do not need to spread hatred, anger, or unkindness. That cycle can stop with us.

Mary's Seven Sorrows are like a school that teaches us how to endure and move through our pain. And remember, no pain is too minor to bring before her. She would often tell the visionaries who encountered her in Kibeho, "I saw that you were not happy today—tell me what happened." In noticing even the smallest brushes with suffering, she encouraged them to speak to her of their troubles in detail so that she could impart the wisdom and care that would help them to bear it.

There is a supernatural aspect of working with the Seven Sorrows Rosary that is inexplicable, for God works in mysterious ways. I know without a doubt that if I hadn't been able to speak to God about my pain around the genocide, I wouldn't be here today. It is our responsibility to faithfully show up for our healing with an open heart and without any desire to retaliate against those who have wronged us. Today I understand that my willingness to share my trials is part and parcel of my salvation.

Before we go any further, I want to clarify that accepting our suffering is not the same as loving it, or as condoning the evil that people have done to us. Often, people believe that if we accept suffering, we are inviting even more of it, or exposing ourselves to continued difficulties. However, in accepting suffering, we lessen it—and when we offer it to Jesus, who is almighty, our yoke becomes much lighter and easier to carry.

When we accept suffering, we allow ourselves to work through a painful, uncomfortable situation without the burden of fear or hatred. We look for solutions rather than looking for someone to blame. The quicker we face our sufferings, the quicker we find a way out. The more we run away from them, the bigger they grow. The more we reject them, the longer they last.

If you are going through a hard situation, I urge you to pray and meditate on the Seven Sorrows and the lessons and stories in this book, which will guide you into a deeper understanding of the prayer's gifts and promises. Find solace in Our Lady and Our Lord. Remember Mary's unwavering faith, despite all she endured. As a mediator of God's grace, she was the person closest to Jesus, and the one who intercedes on our behalf so that we can experience eternal salvation and the full extent of God's love for us.

She wants to come to your aid. She wants you to understand the enormity of God's love for you. She wants you to know that your suffering is a blessing in disguise. She wants you to know that whatever cross you are bearing, you have the strength to carry it—for she is always with you, reminding you that hope can be redeemed at the darkest hour.

*Rooting for you,*

*Immaculée*

# PART I

# THE HISTORY

## OF THE

# SEVEN SORROWS

## CHAPTER 1

# THE ORIGINAL MESSENGER: ST. BRIDGET OF SWEDEN

Before I can share with you the tremendous importance of the Seven Sorrows Rosary, I want to give you a glimpse into the life of the incredible St. Bridget of Sweden (born in 1303; died in 1373). She was the first person to receive this prayer from Our Mother herself. St. Bridget is one of the few Catholic saints to hail from Scandinavia. She was known as the Mystic of the North, and as a pious and wealthy woman, she built the great religious order known as the Brigittines. Her life was centered not only on offering sacred space to the religious visions with which she was gifted from early childhood but also on bringing comfort to the sick and destitute.

Today, Bridget is one of the patron saints of Europe, alongside St. Teresa Benedicta of the Cross and St. Catherine of Siena, who were also pious female saints who devoted their lives to helping and uplifting others, and to putting an end to the religious and political strife that swept through Europe, particularly during the Middle Ages.

St. Bridget was known for putting her riches to generous use. She was born into a wealthy family, and her father, a governor, used his money to help the poor and downtrodden, and to champion fair and just treatment of all people. As a young woman,

Bridget married into the Swedish royal family and raised eight children of her own, including St. Catherine of Sweden. Bridget and her husband also built a hospital on their estate that was open to anyone in dire need.

It was when Bridget's husband died that she took her holy vows—by founding a monastery in which both men and women prayed together but lived in separate quarters. These were the Brigittines, also known as the Order of the Most Holy Savior.

At one point in her life, Bridget learned that an epidemic was afoot in Rome, so without hesitation she went on a pilgrimage to care for the sick and dying. She never returned to Sweden after this. In Rome, as she recognized many systems that worked to keep the poor and downtrodden under a brutal regime, she bravely spoke out against injustice with words so inspiring that they reached the ears of Church officials, including the pope.

Bridget also made a pilgrimage to Jerusalem, the Holy Land, to walk in Our Lord's footsteps and visit the places where he lived, taught, died, and was resurrected. Bridget had received visions of saints, the Blessed Virgin, and Jesus himself throughout her life, so it was no surprise that she continued to experience a number of visitations during prayer visions.

Bridget died when she returned to Rome after this pilgrimage, and her remains were returned to her homeland. She is buried at the monastery that she founded. While many saints might wait several decades—even centuries—to be declared saints, Bridget had to wait only 18 years after her death.

Although most of the Brigittine monasteries across Scandinavia were demolished during the Protestant Reformation, some chapels were built across Europe to honor St. Bridget. The Brigittine order died out completely during the Protestant Reformation, but in 1940 it was revived by Elisabeth Hesselblad, who created a center for women monastics. The new order also has a convent in Rome, known as the Casa di Santa Brigida, which is very close to an area where Bridget lived while she was staying in Rome. The Brigittine sisters also have missions across the world: in Eastern Europe, the Middle East, India, and the United States (in Darien,

Connecticut). Every July 23, we honor St. Bridget and offer to her our prayers, including the prayer to be of service to our neighbors with the same love, care, and dedication that she offered. Bridget was born in 1303 and died on July 23, 1373.

## BRIDGET'S VISIONS

One of the most extraordinary aspects of St. Bridget is that, while she was committed to being in the world and directly responding to its sufferings with dedicated service, she received mystical visions of Jesus, Mary, and a number of saints throughout her lifetime. While many of us are under the impression that the saints who were mystics were cloistered from the world and primarily engaged with sacred contemplation, Bridget's multifaceted identity as a mystic and as an ardent social activist set her apart. She entered a monastery after her husband died.

Bridget's mother died when she was only 10 years old. Bridget was the eldest of three children. After the children were sent to a maternal aunt to continue their childhood education, Bridget had one of her most important early visions in a dream, of the Man of Sorrows—Jesus covered in the wounds he bore on Good Friday. Innocent Bridget asked who had been so cruel as to hurt him in this way. He responded, "All those who despise my love." Bridget was haunted by this vision, which likely determined her religious path at an early age.

### *The Revelations of Our Mother*

In receiving Our Mother's Seven Sorrows, Bridget became an intimate witness to Mary's experience of the crucifixion of her son, and of the great responsibility that she willingly took on in becoming the Mother of God. The words offered by Mary are startling in their level of detail: "My daughter, consider the suffering of my son, for his limbs were like my own limbs and his heart like my own heart. For just as other children used to be carried in the womb of their mother, so was he in me. But he was conceived through the burning charity of God's love. Others, however, are conceived through the lust of the flesh. Thus, John the Evangelist, his cousin, rightly says: 'The word was made flesh.' He came through love and was in me. The word and love created him in me. He was truly for me like my own heart. For when I gave birth to him, I felt as though half my heart was born and went out of me. And when he endured suffering, it felt like my own heart was suffering. Just as when something is half inside and half outside— the half outside feels pain and suffering, but the inside also feels a similar pain—so it was for me when my son was scourged and wounded; it was as if my own heart was scourged and wounded."

Though St. Bridget received the Seven Sorrows and their promises, as well as the request of Our Lady to honor her sorrows, the Order of Servites (Servants of Mary) are the ones who carried forth this legacy and introduced the Seven Sorrows of Mary as a rosary. The order began in the 13th century with seven holy men who hailed from aristocratic families in Florence, Italy, and left of their own accord to live in community on Mount Senario, in solitude and prayer. In fact, it was the Servites to whom Mary appeared and spoke of her wish to be honored as the Mother of Sorrows. The entire raison d'être of the order was to meditate upon the Passion of Jesus and the Seven Sorrows of Mary, and to spread this devotion to the world. This devotion resulted in the Chaplet of the Seven Sorrows of the Blessed Virgin Mary.

As Our Mother told St. Bridget, very few people in the world remembered her Seven Sorrows, much less chose to meditate on them. Our Lady proclaimed to the devout Bridget, "I look around at all who are on earth, to see if by chance there are any who pity me, and meditate upon my sorrows; and I find that there are very few. Therefore, my daughter, though I am forgotten by many, at least do you not forget me; consider my anguish, and imitate, as far as you can, my grief."

I offer deep gratitude to St. Bridget and the Servites for their gifts to the world—for in helping us to remember Mary and her suffering, they have provided us with an effective way of alleviating our own suffering and reconnecting with God.

## CHAPTER 2

# THE WORLD MESSENGER: MARIE-CLAIRE of KIBEHO, RWANDA

In November 2001, the Church, in a very rare move, officially approved the apparitions of the Virgin Mary seen in the 1980s by three schoolgirls in Kibeho, Rwanda: Alphonsine, Anathalie, and Marie-Claire. The girls were tested and examined rigorously by doctors, scientists, psychiatrists, and theologians. Yet no testing could explain the miraculous and supernatural events that occurred when the Blessed Mother appeared to the girls. The evidence of a true apparition was irrefutable, and the local bishop said that there was no doubt a miracle had occurred in Rwanda. Thus, the Vatican endorsed the apparitions of the Virgin Mary in Kibeho to be true, supernatural in nature, and authentic from heaven.

To date, the Church has acknowledged only what Alphonsine, Anathalie, and Marie-Claire witnessed between 1981 and 1989. However, several other visionaries saw both the Virgin Mary and Jesus, and they were also studied by the same team of investigators; many of them continue to have apparitions, and it is my hope that their messages will someday also be approved. Tens of thousands of onlookers—many of them priests and people of science—witnessed the apparitions of at least five of these other visionaries. I was among the earliest believers that Mary and Jesus had come to Rwanda. However, long before Father Rwagema, my village's local priest, began traveling to Kibeho to tape the visionaries' messages, I knew in my heart that our country had been touched by a divine power.

Among the aspects that mark the uniqueness of the apparitions of Kibeho, we find the Seven Sorrows Rosary of the Virgin Mary. While the rosary dates back to the Middle Ages, it gained new popularity following the Marian apparitions in Kibeho. We were taught this rosary by the Virgin Mary herself when she appeared to her intermediary, 21-year-old Marie-Claire Mukangango. In one of Mary's apparitions to Marie-Claire, she assigned the young visionary a mission to reintroduce this special prayer to the world. Marie-Claire then asked Our Lady how she can teach the whole world since she didn't have much money to travel even to the next city. The Virgin Mary smiled at her and said, "Don't worry, my child, you do what you can; the grace of God is almighty. I have many children in the world, you know." Marie-Claire never asked again; she did her part, traveled the country to teach it to thousands of people, who then taught it to thousands of others. Sadly, Marie-Claire's life was cut short; she was killed in the genocide against Tutsis back in 1994, of more than a million people in Rwanda, a tragedy that was foretold through visions of rivers of blood that the young visionaries in Kibeho received several years before the killings. Despite Marie-Claire's untimely death, the gift she brought to the world is incomparable—and even through the ensuing years of horror in Rwanda and elsewhere, her impact continues to be felt in powerful ways.

## WHEN THE APPARITIONS BEGAN

My country was truly a peaceful paradise, especially during the early 1980s, when Rwanda's miraculous events inspired a national feeling of brotherly love and a renewal of belief and faith in God.

The shrine for Our Lady of Kibeho has become a place of worship and prayer for hundreds of thousands of pilgrims from all over Africa and the world, many of whom claimed miraculous healings at the site—yet most of the world hasn't heard about this blessed place.

In those days, our family didn't have a television or even a telephone, so our spare time was usually spent together. One night, as we were finishing dinner, Dad began telling us about how he'd visited Father Clement that day in our neighboring parish. Father Clement was the most revered priest in the region, as well as a deeply pious, well-educated, and wise man. He was also a good family friend. While he was especially close to my father, my brothers and I loved him so much that we called him Grandpa.

"A priest in Kibeho let Clement know about a 16-year-old girl named Alphonsine Mumureke, who says the Virgin Mary appeared to her at least five times in the past two weeks," Dad told us. "The girl claims that the Blessed Mother wants to be known in Rwanda as the 'Mother of the Word,' and that God Almighty sent her here with messages from heaven for the entire world to hear."

It turned out that we weren't the only family discussing Alphonsine's apparitions. Within days, the name Alphonsine Mumureke was on the lips of everyone in our village. The story of her apparitions had traveled overnight from tiny Kibeho to Rwanda's capital city, Kigali. People discussed her visions on Radio Rwanda, and they even made news in our neighboring countries of Burundi, Tanzania, Zaire (now the Democratic Republic of the Congo), and Uganda. Her photographs and story also appeared in a famous magazine, *Jeune Afrique*, or "Young Africa."

Peasants around Kibeho were leaving their fields and milling about at the girls' school hoping to see an apparition or a sign in the sky. News of the Virgin's arrival had moved so quickly across the country that I considered it a miracle in and of itself. The days and times Mary would come to Alphonsine were announced beforehand to her, and although the young visionary never issued an announcement on the radio, the news would travel the country in a matter of hours and people made long trips to Kibeho so they could be present during the apparitions. In addition, many people shared their own accounts of being touched by the apparitions; they reported seeing signs in the sky or being touched in supernatural healing ways.

I'd already asked Mary to make Rwandans believe that she'd arrived, and now the whole nation knew she'd come! But as I discovered later through my own research, Mary had arrived in Rwanda decades before, as if to prepare the way for a more tangible arrival.

It was Sister Theresa Kamugisha, the Mother Superior of the Benebikira religious order in Rwanda from 1953–64, who received visions of Mary. The Benebikira Sisters were founded in the early 1900s and were envisioned as an opportunity to build a native Rwandan congregation that would intersperse our cultural practices with service and devotion. They were known for providing education, particularly for girls, and caring for the sick and poor, especially women and children. They evangelized by example, infusing their acts of service with justice, love, and the ability to see God in all things. In Kinyarwanda, the language of my country, their name means "Daughters of Mary."

Sister Theresa was a remarkable woman who encouraged the women of Rwanda to give their lives to God in full faith—and to be more resilient, independent, and responsible for the salvation of their people. Although Sister Theresa didn't have the privilege of much education, she valued learning and was able to garner a number of scholarships for herself and her sisters from a number of European congregations. Sister Theresa lived through a time of great change and political discord in Rwanda; in 1962, Rwanda gained its independence and was separated from Burundi. Afterward, violence quickly ensued between the Tutsi and Hutu people. The Tutsis were exiled and attacked, while the Hutus responded with slaughter. Throughout this ethnic divide, the Benebikira Sisters lived in a state of unity and peace, their order reflecting the harmony of God's will for us.

It was in 1954 that Sister Theresa had her first vision of Mary. Incredibly, she received the instruction to teach the sisters in the order the Seven Sorrows Rosary. Sister Theresa asked, "Do you mean for me to teach the children in our school the rosary as well?" Mary responded that this would not be necessary, as she herself planned to come back to teach it not only to the students but the entire world.

While Sister Theresa faithfully obeyed Mary and taught the other sisters the forgotten prayer, another superior who came along after she departed didn't emphasize the importance of fidelity to the rosary. The order dropped the habit of saying this prayer altogether—until that fateful day when Our Lady appeared to Marie-Claire.

## MARIE-CLAIRE, SKEPTIC TURNED BELIEVER

Marie-Claire was an unexpected visionary. In the early 1980s, Mary first appeared to the schoolgirls Alphonsine and Anathalie at Benebikira High School (which had been established in 1967) in Kibeho. While many at the high school were convinced, plenty remained doubtful. The school director, who'd assumed Alphonsine was mentally ill, now worried that her school had become a target for the devil.

Marie-Claire, always Alphonsine's greatest detractor, declared war on Anathalie as well, accusing the two girls of forming a diabolical plot to gain national attention. She began spying on Anathalie and Alphonsine, reading their letters and diaries when they were away from the dorm, and watching them closely day and night for signs of collusion. Because of this, Alphonsine and Anathalie avoided each other so as not to draw suspicion or accusation. And while both girls continued to receive regular apparitions, they always took place at different times.

Marie-Claire was so incensed by what was happening that she personally complained about the "false visionaries" to the head of the local archdiocese, Bishop Jean-Baptiste Gahamanyi. When the bishop told the impetuous girl that he'd already spoken to Alphonsine and that the situation was being monitored,

Marie-Claire only became angrier. She worked herself into such a state over the mischievous "scam" Alphonsine and Anathalie were perpetrating under the bishop's nose that she vowed not to rest until she'd unmasked their fakery. And if any student was in a position to debunk and humiliate the visionaries, it was Marie-Claire Mukangango.

Marie-Claire entered the world in 1961 in one of the poorest areas of southern Rwanda, and she was a born fighter. Her father died a few months after her birth, and her mother often had difficulty providing for her, so Marie-Claire lived with her grandparents for much of her childhood. Perhaps because she had an unstable home life as a child, Marie-Claire learned to fend for herself early on and didn't let people push her around or take advantage of her. And she never felt sorry for herself; rather, she was independent, saucy, bright, charming, and charismatic. Raised Catholic, she believed in God, the saints, and all the sacraments that are part and parcel of a Catholic upbringing, but she wasn't very religious. Sitting in church was not her favorite pastime. In fact, she had a hard time sitting anywhere for any length of time. She was brimming with energy and grew fidgety and restless when kept indoors. She'd rather be running around a soccer field or out dancing—which she loved with a passion—than be stuck in a classroom or attending a prayer meeting with the other girls.

Marie-Claire was indeed loudmouthed, obstinate, and often rude; however, she was also open and honest, which tended to make people trust her. And while she could be sharply critical of those who annoyed or offended her, her quick wit kept her friends laughing and in good spirits. She loved to talk and debate with friends, and she won most arguments she engaged in with the sheer force of her personality—if Marie-Claire was convinced she was right about something, no one could prove her wrong. Her self-confidence and outgoing nature made her popular, even admired. She was voted class president by her schoolmates year after year because they knew she'd always speak up for them; she wasn't afraid to stand up to any of the teachers, nuns, and priests who ruled Rwanda's Catholic school system. And she certainly wasn't afraid to stand up to Alphonsine and Anathalie, or anyone else who supported their status as visionaries.

Even though Marie-Claire wasn't very devout, she did pray to the Virgin Mary and was offended that anyone would be shameless enough to use the Holy Mother to win popularity and favor with others. She began praying the rosary to ask Mary to help her rid the school of the false prophets. By early February, Marie-Claire's campaign of ridicule and harassment against the two young seers had become so nasty that even a priest who'd asked her to torment and discredit Alphonsine months earlier now cautioned the young woman not to be so mean. But Marie-Claire had a stubborn streak, so it would take more than a priest's scolding for her to look kindly upon Alphonsine and Anathalie. It would take a miracle.

The miracle began on March 1, 1982, when Marie-Claire fainted during a walk in the garden between classes. A few minutes later, she came to—or so she thought. Instead of being outside in the sunshine, she found herself in the dark with no idea where she was. The air stank with the odor of human waste and decaying flesh so disgusting she wanted to vomit. She got to her feet and ran blindly through the darkness, hoping that she was heading toward the school. She banged into the main door, and when she flung it open, the putrid stench disappeared and the daylight returned. She ran into the dormitory and found herself standing in front of Alphonsine, who was having an apparition and chatting amicably with the Holy Mother.

Marie-Claire looked down at her clothes and found they were soaking wet. That's when she realized that two classmates were holding her up by her arms and walking her toward her bed. "Did I fall into the stream?" she asked, thinking she must have bashed her head and hallucinated.

The girls gave their friend a strange look and told her they'd found her lying semiconscious in the school chapel. They tried to get her to return to the dorm, but she refused to leave, mumbling that she'd never again set foot in the room where the visionaries had their apparitions.

The two girls ran for help and returned with a nun who carried a large bottle of holy water brought from Lourdes (a town in southwestern France where, in 1858, the Virgin Mary appeared to a local woman). After the nun doused Marie-Claire with the water and said a benediction over her, the girls carried their friend to her room. Marie-Claire had no idea what had happened, except that she'd been unconscious for a good part of the afternoon. She had no answers to offer the many girls who passed by her bed asking about her experience. She was so shaken that evening that she began writing a letter to her mother, saying she'd taken ill and wanted to come home to rest for a while. But she'd written only a few words when she again lost consciousness and was back in the dark; this time, she wasn't alone—two menacing figures approached her from the shadows. Marie-Claire couldn't clearly identify who was standing in front of her, but they hovered in the darkness like specters. When they spoke, their wheezing voices were threatening.

"More of us were supposed to come for you tonight, but they haven't arrived," said one. "But we'll be back. We're never far away," said the other, and then they both vanished. Marie-Claire rubbed her eyes, only to discover that she was on the floor of the school chapel surrounded by classmates, including Alphonsine, who handed her a little statue of Our Lady of Lourdes.

"Keep her with you to protect you from the evil one," Alphonsine said. "Last night when the Blessed Mother appeared to me, she warned me that the devil was planning to attack students at the school. She says that we can protect ourselves from the enemy by wearing our rosaries."

Marie-Claire stared at Alphonsine but didn't say anything. "I will pray for you," Alphonsine added as she left the chapel.

"I don't need prayers from her," Marie-Claire told the other girls, and then asked them how she'd ended up in the chapel again.

They told their friend that she'd dropped her pencil while writing, and when she bent down to retrieve it, she'd fallen off the bed and had a fit or seizure—her body had flailed about wildly, her eyes rolled back into her head, and her tongue hung out of her mouth. The girls had tried to help but could do nothing, and when the fit ended, Marie-Claire had run to the chapel and collapsed.

Marie-Claire shook her head in disbelief and looked down at the statue Alphonsine had given her. "All of this is the fault of those phony visionaries. I told you they'd bring us trouble. If demons are haunting this school, it's because of Alphonsine's voo-doo!" she replied angrily.

The next morning, March 2, the girls were in their religious studies class learning about the Holy Mother's appearances in 1917 to the children of Fátima in Portugal. As part of the lesson, the nun—one of the few members of the faculty who believed Alphonsine and Anathalie to be true visionaries—instructed the girls to sing a beautiful Rwandan hymn, "Ibisiza n'Imisozi."

All Rwandan girls love singing—and singing in class, especially about the Holy Mother, could be a real treat. The young ladies jumped to their feet, clapping their hands and stamping their feet to bring energy and life to the old hymn:

*Ibisiza n'imisozi, bitaratangira kuremwa,*
*Imana yari igufite, mu bitekerezo byayo.*
(Before the mountains and valleys were created,
God had you in mind, Mother.)

*Kuva aho isi igera hose, mu bantu bose bo kwi usi,*
*Baririmba Imakulata, uwo Imana yagize imanzi.*
(The whole world sings the Immaculate Conception,
the one God chose to be the Mother of his Son).

Halfway through the song, Anathalie told the nun that her skin was tingling, which was a sign the Blessed Mother was about to appear to her. She asked permission to go to the chapel, which the nun immediately granted, telling the rest of the girls to go with their schoolmate and keep singing the entire way.

Marie-Claire, who sat behind Anathalie in class, followed reluctantly at the back of the line. She thought that the nun was out of line and hated seeing the visionaries being encouraged.

And as soon as they entered the close quarters of the small chapel, the young woman became very uncomfortable as the panic and fear of the previous day's blackouts rushed back to her. She bolted for the door but lost consciousness before making it outside. As she'd already done twice within 24 hours, she opened her eyes and found herself somewhere she didn't recognize. This time, she wasn't in the dark, though—she was standing beneath the most clear, shining blue sky in an open field of perfectly manicured, sweet-smelling grass. Each blade bent from the weight of fat drops of dew that caught colors of the sky like a million crystal prisms. The light that shone on them was out of this world; though it was brighter than the sun, it was easy to look at it.

Marie-Claire caught her breath. It was the prettiest thing she'd ever seen. But the beauty didn't calm her down. She could think of two explanations for what was happening to her, and neither was good: either she was going insane, or the devil had taken possession of her senses. Then, out of nowhere, a soft voice called out her last name. "Mukangango." Marie-Claire spun around, her fists clenched and poised in front of her like a boxer. She thought that the specters who'd accosted her the previous night had returned to finish her off. She looked around in every direction but saw only the endless sea of shimmering grass. She responded wordlessly to the voice by raising her fists higher and planting her feet firmly on the grass.

"Mukangango," the voice called again.

No one had ever said Marie-Claire's name so sweetly. The tender voice, like that of a loving mother, was as soothing as a lullaby. But the girl was distrustful and answered the voice with a challenge: "Okay, you've found me. I am Mukangango. I'm here, and I'm ready to fight!"

With an affectionate laugh, the voice asked, "Why would you want to fight me, my child? What is making you so afraid? Never be afraid of your mother!"

At that moment, Marie-Claire realized with certainty that it was the Holy Mother who was speaking to her. None of the students or staff present at Kibeho High School on March 2, 1982, ever forgot the atmosphere on campus that night. Word spread in a matter of minutes that Marie-Claire, the sworn enemy and most outspoken critic of the school's two visionaries, had confessed that she, too, had been visited by the Holy Mother.

Many students described watching Marie-Claire enter a state of ecstasy in the school chapel, hold hands with the visionary Anathalie, and sing to the Blessed Virgin. She then collapsed on the floor in such a mental fog that she had to be carried to her bed. The story was told a hundred times by each of the 30 witnesses, each time from a different perspective and with slight variations in the details. But every version had an identical central theme: the Marie-Claire who'd walked into the chapel that morning was not the same Marie-Claire who'd been carried out.

The young woman was in a constant state of prayer after her apparition, kneeling for hours and praying the rosary, begging the Holy Mother for forgiveness. She recanted every accusation she'd made about Alphonsine and Anathalie, and swore that she'd devote her life to serving God. Her rude, brusque, and aggressive manner had vanished overnight, and, as passing years would prove, would never return. Soon, Marie-Claire became the person who willingly helped her classmates—washing clothes for sick students and offering words and deeds of kindness whenever she could. It was the dramatic change in her character that convinced many Rwandans of the veracity of the apparitions.

Marie-Claire was a perfect example of the spiritual conversion the Blessed Mother had been calling for since first appearing to Alphonsine. No, Marie-Claire wasn't an incorrigible sinner, but like so many Rwandans (and like so many people everywhere in the world) she'd been too preoccupied with the distractions of life to focus on the spiritual needs of the soul. Miracles had been happening in front of the girl for months, but she'd been so focused on exposing lies that she'd missed the truth.

Later, she said that life would have been much easier and more spiritually rewarding for her if, instead of channeling her energy and time to discrediting Alphonsine and Anathalie, she'd stopped for a moment and really listened to the messages.

After one apparition, Marie-Claire commented that one of Our Lady's greatest sorrows during her many visits to Kibeho was that not enough people truly listened to the loving advice and counsel she offered through her visionaries. Too many individuals came to the village simply to witness a miracle, and while their eyes and ears searched the heavens for a supernatural event, their hearts failed to hear the messages Mary repeated again and again: love God, love and be kind to each other, read the Bible, follow God's commandments, accept the love of Jesus Christ, repent for sins, be humble, seek and offer forgiveness, and live the gift of your life how God wants you to—with a clean and open heart and a clear conscience. Mary especially emphasized the power of prayer, often repeating the word *pray* three times to speak of its importance. She said, "My children, I don't know how to help you if you can't pray. Pray, pray, and pray. It is crucial to pray, for your souls cannot be at peace without prayer."

## THE ROSARY OF THE SEVEN SORROWS

In the months after Marie-Claire's first apparition, during which she could only hear Mary, the Blessed Mother began appearing to the novice visionary many times a week.

The Virgin had a nickname for Marie-Claire that showed she had a soft spot for the visionary. Mary loved the girl's open nature, childlike naivete, and great passion for life—a passion so great that Marie-Claire became the only person in recorded history to challenge the Blessed Mother to a fist fight! Whatever the reason, Mary's nickname for Marie-Claire was "the Cherished of the Blessed Mother," and she often favored the seer by granting her requests. (The nickname reveals Mary's sense of humor, as it was derived from a name Marie-Claire's father used to call her: the "Cherished of Daddy." Mary adopted part of the nickname to make the young girl laugh and to feel loved—for not only was she cherished by Daddy, she was also cherished by Our Mother!)

For example, Marie-Claire once asked if her sister, who'd died a year before, was in heaven. The Virgin replied that she was in a place of suffering—she was in purgatory, waiting to be allowed into heaven.

When Marie-Claire actually saw the Blessed Mother, she said that Mary descended to her from heaven on a soft silver cloud. Like Alphonsine, Marie-Claire claimed that the Queen of Heaven was a young woman who exuded warm, motherly love; that her skin was neither white nor black; and that she was wearing a seamless white dress with a white veil covering her hair. Marie-Claire further shared that the lady was carrying a black rosary unlike any she'd seen before, which the Mother of God told her was an ancient one called "the Rosary of the Seven Sorrows." The rosary held deep meaning for Mary, who said that she'd soon teach Marie-Claire how to pray this special prayer, and that it would be the girl's mission in life to reintroduce it to the world. Just like Anathalie had, Marie-Claire accepted her mission without hesitation.

It was on March 3, 1982, that the Virgin Mary spoke to Marie-Claire for the first time about the prayer of the Seven Sorrows Rosary. As Marie-Claire explained it, the purpose of this rosary was to help us meditate on the Passion of Jesus and the great sorrows of his mother. When recited properly, it can open our hearts and redirect us away from sin, as it is sin that ultimately put Jesus on the cross. There is a process of inner conversion that occurs when we meditate on the mysteries of the Seven Sorrows, and when we join in the suffering of Mary and her beloved son.

On May 31, 1982, the Blessed Virgin reminded Marie-Claire of the true power of her message by saying, "What I ask you is to ask for forgiveness. If you recite this rosary by meditating, you'll find in you the strength to return to God. These days, people no longer know how to ask for forgiveness. They continue to crucify the Son of God."

Our Lady gave Marie-Claire the Seven Sorrows Rosary to help her spread it to the whole world. At first, Marie-Claire was reluctant. She said, "Mother, you want me to teach the whole world the Seven Sorrows Rosary? I don't even have the money to go to the next city. How do you expect me to teach the whole world?" Our Lady replied, "My child, my grace can do all things. I have many children in the world. You do your part, and the grace of God will take it to the next person."

During this time of the Marian apparitions and the revelation of the Seven Sorrows Rosary, Father Clement made the observation that suddenly everyone had become much kinder. When my brother Damascene returned from his first pilgrimage to Kibeho, for instance, he immediately joined the Legion of Mary and began visiting the sick and elderly in our region. My eldest brother, Aimable, was more gracious with his time and spent hours helping me with schoolwork, and as I mentioned in the Introduction to this book, our father single-handedly built a small wooden chapel where people could pray the Seven Sorrows Rosary and the traditional rosary.

"The Blessed Mother told Marie-Claire that she wanted everyone to learn and pray with it as often as possible," Dad explained as I watched him hammer the chapel together, board by board, nail by nail. "People will want to say Our Lady's special prayer more often if they have a special place to do it in."

One night, a radio program rebroadcast an apparition in which Marie-Claire shared the message my father had been referring to. The young lady repeated what the Blessed Mother had told her word for word: "What I am asking you to do is to repent. If you say the Rosary of the Seven Sorrows and meditate on it well, you will find all the strength you need to repent of your sins and convert your heart. The world has become deaf and cannot hear the truth of the word. Today people no longer know how to apologize for the wrong they do through sin; they put the Son of God on the cross again and again. That is why I have come here. I have come to remind the world—and especially you here in Rwanda, where I still can find humble souls and people who are not attached to money or wealth—to hear my words and find repentance."

*Wow, I've got to get one of those special rosaries!* I thought. I prayed for Mary to send me one, and she did (through my dad) a week later. Father Clement told me that the seven medals on this rosary represented each of the Seven Sorrows of Mary. The First Sorrow was when a holy man named Simeon told Mary that her newborn son would change the world but suffer greatly, and that her son's suffering would pain her like a sword stuck into her heart. The Second Sorrow was the dangerous flight Mary, Joseph, and Jesus made to live as exiles in Egypt when Jesus was being hunted by King Herod's death squads. The Third Sorrow was when 12-year-old Jesus was lost in Jerusalem for three days. The Fourth Sorrow was when Mary witnessed her son's agony on his way to Calvary. The Fifth Sorrow was watching Jesus suffer on the cross. The Sixth Sorrow was receiving her son's body as it was lowered from the cross. Finally, Mary's Seventh Sorrow was placing her beloved son in a tomb.

As far away as I was from Kibeho, when I prayed with my rosary, meditating deeply on the story associated with each medal, I felt the Holy Mother kneeling beside me. The love she felt for her son, as well as her suffering as a mother, overwhelmed me. The magnitude of her sacrifice was beyond my comprehension and made all my childish concerns and complaints seem petty in comparison. But the strength of her love, which I could see reflected in each tale, is what truly moved me.

Mary knew who her son was, and from his earliest days was aware of the pain that awaited him (and her). Yet, through all those years, she supported him with the love of a mother, standing by him while he was whipped, beaten, and crucified. And she was there for him when he drew his last breath. I realized that Our Lady, whose soft and gentle voice enthralled the visionaries, had rock-solid strength. It was the rock upon which I would build my faith in God, the strength that would sustain me through whatever sorrows life held in store for me. I didn't know it then, but this vow I made would serve me in dramatic ways in the years to come.

The chapel my dad built was open to people of all religions, and the doors were never locked. Mary's message about learning to pray her special rosary was the one he most took to heart. Thus, the last nail he hammered into the wall of the chapel was used to tack up a list of instructions on how to pray the rosary as the Blessed

Virgin had taught Marie-Claire. He spent a great deal of time at the chapel himself, and not just praying the rosary—because most people in the village couldn't read, he'd have to explain the instructions he posted. Pilgrims from northern Rwanda passed through our town, Mataba, every day, and Dad made sure that we were as hospitable to them as the kind strangers he'd encountered walking to Kibeho had been. It seemed the entire country was on the move; everyone was in a hurry to get to Kibeho because no one knew when the visions might end.

The public apparitions of the Virgin Mary to Marie-Claire ended on September 15, 1982, which is, coincidentally, the day when the Church commemorates Our Lady of Sorrows. It became clear that the mission to which Marie-Claire had been assigned was complete. Mary told the young seer, "Given that many people know already the Rosary of Sorrows, and in case they wanted, they may now know, we will not meet anymore in the presence of a big crowd. Of course, I'll come back from time to time to visit you and remind you of one thing or another, but this shall happen now in private."

This was not an easy thing for Marie-Claire to hear. In front of thousands of people, she cried bitterly. Her ensuing apparitions came by surprise and lasted only a short time. Marie-Claire knew she would never be with Mary for very long periods ever again, and it broke her heart. People who were present when Marie-Claire said good-bye to Mary were just as heartbroken. Although Marie-Claire would cry over this loss for months to come, Mary had promised the girl that she would never leave her alone for a moment, and that even without words or direct contact, she would always watch over her.

On the day of the final public apparition, Marie-Claire asked Mary what her mission in life would be and expressed her desire to become a nun. However, Our Mother told Marie-Claire that she was not called to such a vocation. This was another sword through Marie-Claire's heart. Later she would express to the members of the commission investigating the Kibeho apparitions that she was saddened to think that Mary didn't believe she was capable of being a nun. The Bishop of Kibeho attempted to comfort her. He once said, "Whenever she spoke about this, she cried very hard, to the point that I would stop interviewing her as a judge but would start to console her as a father . . . trying to find reasons why Mary said that . . . maybe because God had better plans for her." One time she asked the Virgin Mary for a gift to show her father. The Virgin Mary accepted and only showed her his feet. She cried and said, "Oh those are his feet, Mother. How happy I am to see even his feet alone." She then asked Mary why she couldn't see his whole body. Mary told her that she would see him whole when she comes to heaven.

## THE TRAGEDY OF THE RWANDAN GENOCIDE

Of course, among the beautiful visions and prayers that Marie-Claire shared with the world, there were also many warnings and prophecies of difficulties to come. Marie-Claire continually wailed at the images she was shown—of streets coursing with blood and corpses—and she begged Rwandans to heed Mary's pleas and warnings before it was too late: "Our Lady says, 'Do not forget that God is more powerful than all the evil in the world . . . the world is on the edge of catastrophe. Cleanse your hearts through prayer. The only way is God. If you don't take refuge in God, where will you go to hide when the fire has spread everywhere?'"

Unfortunately, not enough people prayed; too few cleansed their hearts of hatred. For the few who did change, Our Lady promised that Rwanda would rise again, and it would be a light that would bring many to pray on that land, in Kibeho.

The fire did indeed come, and there was nowhere to hide for more than a million innocent souls whose bodies were chopped to pieces during the genocide that engulfed Rwanda in the spring of 1994. Thousands upon thousands of bodies were dumped into rivers that ran thick with human blood. It was Alphonsine who had received this apocalyptic vision of rivers of blood, which was so horrifically accurate that Mary's messages would eventually be believed and accepted by everyone from the peasants to the pope. But by that time, it was too late.

Marie-Claire, who'd married and moved to Kigali in 1987 to teach, ran to the aid of her husband just as killers were dragging him away during the genocide in 1994. The murderers then turned on Marie-Claire, the feisty woman who had once challenged the Holy Mother to a fist fight, and she was slain on the spot.

Marie-Claire will never be forgotten, though. The gift of her courage and faith still remains with us. Heaven sent its Queen to Kibeho and its young seers to bring us messages of truth and teach us the power of love and faith. That power still radiates through the sky and in the ground, as well as in the hearts of all those who make the pilgrimage to this holy place.

## CHAPTER 3

# MARY'S CHAPELS

There is something about being in a building where the devotion of countless people has consecrated the space that is unlike any other experience I can think of. Churches are meant to be sacred sites, places of refuge that radiate an all-powerful light with the power to shepherd us back home. Here, people converse with God and give to him all that is heavy in their hearts, unburdening themselves of suffering and festering secrets. If we have ever felt lost, alone, or dejected, there is always a church to remind us that God is here among us, gently beckoning us back to his flock.

A church is also a place where we can safely hear God's word, pray, and meditate on his mysteries. When we connect to such a place, we maintain his covenant, and we solidify both our faith and our connection to a community that holds him at its center. There are numerous stories about the potency of these holy places, which are often gorgeously crafted to mirror the awe-inspiring beauty of the divine. It is little wonder that so many people have experienced visitations from Our Lord, as well as the Blessed Virgin, with exhortations to build churches on the hallowed ground where they have appeared.

Many decades ago, when Our Lady appeared to Sister Theresa, she asked her to build a small chapel on the land, using specific measurements, and to place within it the images of her Seven Sorrows. It was said that Mary literally came down from heaven and walked the ground herself. With the supervision of Sister Theresa, the chapel was built in the rural village of Save, where the first Catholic church in Rwanda was erected. It is there that Sister Theresa's body is buried.

One of the nuns in Save told me that during the genocide, 250 nuns, both Tutsi and Hutu, took shelter in the chapel. The people who were on a murderous rampage knew that the nuns were there. Every other day, they went to see and hurl insults at them, but for some reason they did not kill them. One day, they never came back. During the three months of the genocide waged against Tutsis, the nuns prayed together from sunup to sundown and said the Seven Sorrows Rosary in the Chapel of the Seven Sorrows. It is said that anyone who prays in this chapel receives answers to their prayers. I regularly visit the chapel whenever I make pilgrimages to Kibeho.

Through her visionaries in Kibeho, Mary also requested that her followers build two chapels in Kibeho in memory of her apparitions; these would also be places in which to remember and pray the Seven Sorrows Rosary. In November 1993, the Chapel of the Apparitions was created by transforming one of the dormitories from the high school where the three primary visionaries first saw Mary. Tragically, during the Rwandan genocide, not even the beloved visionaries of Kibeho were spared from the carnage. Terrible massacres took place in 1994—both in the Kibeho parish church, as well as the esplanade where the apparitions had occurred. During this time, those who remembered the visionaries' prophecies of "headless corpses floating down the river" wept to see such a sacred site desecrated. In 2001, the apparitions of Kibeho were approved by the Vatican, and right before the cardinal came to anoint the place, a chapel was built in honor of the apparitions—right next to the small Chapel of the Apparitions.

It is little wonder that the beautiful shrine is designed around the number seven, which number Mary's sorrows. The number seven is sacred in scripture. In Christian doctrine, seven often symbolizes perfection and spiritual realization. For example, God created heaven and earth in six days and rested on the seventh day. Jesus made seven statements on the cross. He also offered seven metaphors describing the path of salvation. These beautiful metaphors are: the bread of life (John 6:35); the light of the world (John 8:12); the gate to salvation (John 10:9); the good shepherd (John 10:11); the resurrection and the life (John 11:25–26); the way, the truth, and the life (John 14:6); and the vine (John 15:5). The Lord's Prayer contains seven petitions. And, of course, Mary's Seven Sorrows symbolize the deep mystery of the experience of suffering, which can lead to spiritual transformation. This is why the structure of the shrine, with its beautiful facade windows, the enormous rosette, and the crosses that adorn the walls, all evoke the presence of the sacred, which is palpable to everyone who goes there: to honor Our Lady, to commemorate and mourn the massacre of so many innocent Rwandans, and to welcome the miracles that have made it such a special and unique destination.

However, the church holds only 500 people at most, while the small chapel next to it holds 25 to 30. Mary specifically told Marie-Claire that she wanted two churches with distinct measurements: a small one that would hold up to 1,000 people and a large one that would hold up to 10,000, with the addition of an outdoor plaza that would hold up to 50,000. Marie-Claire noted that Mary wanted people to know: "All I want is your willingness to help and your love and I will guide the rest."

More than 40 years later, it has not been done.

## MARY'S REQUEST: TWO CHAPELS FOR ALL HER CHILDREN

Years after the genocide, I would come to be acquainted with Mary's requests for two chapels to be built in Kibeho. Marie-Claire was given the gift of the Seven Sorrows Rosary, and she was also given instructions to offer to then-bishop of Butare, Jean-Baptiste Gahamanyi. (Butare is the diocese to which Kibeho belonged during the time of the apparition.) In 1982, Mary told Marie-Claire to inform the bishop that she wanted them to build her two chapels in memory of her apparitions to Kibeho, for all her children who would come to pray to God. Mary promised that this place would be anointed—meaning it would be a place where heaven touched earth. Here, Mary would listen to the prayers of all her children. The entire world was invited to come.

When Marie-Claire took this message to the bishop, he was attending a meeting at which all the bishops of Rwanda were assembled. Marie-Claire relayed the Blessed Virgin's message, and Bishop Gahamanyi shared it with the others. Collectively, they sent a message back to Mary through Marie-Claire: "Tell Mary that we have many chapels in the area. Can she use them instead of having us build new ones?"

Chagrined, Marie-Claire spoke to Mary, who graciously thanked the bishops but sent another message: "Tell my children that I thank them for their suggestions, but tell them that I want new chapels." The bishops came back with yet another message: "Tell Mary that we are poor! We don't have the money to build new chapels. Besides, where would we even build them?" Marie-Claire returned with another message from Mary: "I will not ask any of you for your own money. I have many children in the world, so I will find the money myself. All I ask is that you willingly decide to help in this mission, with your full love and faith." Then they asked Mary through Marie-Claire, "Do you want those chapels to be built in every diocese?" Mary gave Marie-Claire an answer: "Tell them no, I want the chapels to be built here on the place of the apparitions. These chapels will not belong to the diocese of Butare alone but to the whole world, for all my children who will come to pray here. This is a place for them."

Over time, Marie-Claire relayed several messages on Mary's behalf, noting that Mary wanted the chapels to be built in the place where she was continuing to appear to the visionaries.

Although Mary had given clear instructions, the bishops continued to feign ignorance, insisting that they had no idea where they would build the churches or how large they should be.

Amazingly, weeks after Marie-Claire first received the message about the chapels, Mary appeared to one of the other visionaries, Anathalie. During the apparition, which thousands of people (including ones to whom I am still connected many years later) had come to witness, Mary told Anathalie: "I hear them asking themselves where I want the chapels and how big I want them to be. I will show them today." Besides many witnesses who had come to listen to the messages of Our Lady, the investigators from the Catholic Church were also present, and theologians and doctors were busily taking notes. It was a perfect day for witnesses to be present, and I am glad for this, because there would later be many people attempting to misrepresent the messages that were clearly given by Our Lady.

Mary literally took Anathalie from the podium where she stood and made her walk the land while offering a vivid description of the chapels, as if they had already been built. Mary asked Anathalie to take steps from one end to the other. As Anathalie walked, people were able to follow her and measure one large chapel, 60 meters long, and a small one, 30 meters long. Anathalie was clearly entranced by what she saw, as she continued to remark, "Wow, Mother! This is too beautiful. I don't believe anyone will know how to build such a place." She described the statue of Mary and the vivid colors of the chapels, as onlookers—from church officials to laypeople—feverishly took notes. Anathalie described how the chapels were decorated with specific color patterns that seemed to reflect traditional Rwandan designs, although the colors seemed to be gold and silver.

Our Lady told Anathalie that the big chapel would be called "A Reunion of the Dispersed," while the small one would be the "Chapel of the Seven Sorrows." Anathalie described the paintings in the smaller chapel, which depicted each of Mary's Seven Sorrows. Anathalie noted that the paintings were so big and magnificent that they practically filled the entire walls. She mentioned that toward the altar, she could see a hand holding the Seven Sorrows Rosary, but not the whole person. The large chapel contained massive paintings of the Stations of the Cross, a series of images depicting Jesus on his way to Calvary on the day of his crucifixion.

Despite Anathalie's clear descriptions to thousands of people, and the subsequent authentication of the Marian apparitions in Kibeho by the Catholic Church, Mary's requests were met with continued disbelief. Mary often said that wherever she was, Satan would also be there to sow doubt and discord, and she often begged the people to pray so that they would not be confused by Satan's stratagems. As I think about the many years of resistance and stalemates that would ensue, I recognize the work of the devil through many good, well-intentioned people. I know that if the bishops were truly willing to obey Mary's wishes, and if they were willing to surrender to their faith in God, they would have been inspired to take action right away. But this would not be so.


## WHEN THE DIOCESE WAS CUT IN TWO

In 1985, after a few years of psychological, physical, and theological investigations of the visionaries in Kibeho, Bishop Gahamanyi gave the first approval of 11 who'd had apparitions of Mary and Jesus. However, in 1987, the Church announced that the Diocese of Butare would be divided in two. Bishop Baptiste would be given one part, but sadly, Kibeho was taken out of his hands and placed in the Diocese of Gikongoro. At this point, the Diocese of Gikongoro was under the jurisdiction of Bishop Augustin Misago, who would officially make any decisions about Catholic Church activities in Kibeho.

In 2001, the Marian apparitions were officially approved by the Church, although only three of the visionaries (Alphonsine, Anathalie, and Marie-Claire) would be approved by Bishop Misago, and only for the apparitions of the Virgin Mary, not of Jesus, which by the way Anathalie had both the visits of Mary and of Jesus—his declaration that was published by the Vatican. Though

I was sad that Jesus's apparitions were not approved and that the other visionaries approved by the first bishop were not added, at least at this point I was certain that there would be no more excuses for why the chapels could not be built . . . but I was wrong.

If you might recall, a small Chapel of the Apparitions had already been built in 1993 from one of Kibeho High School's dormitories. In 2001, the Vatican sent a cardinal to anoint a new church to honor the apparitions, so Bishop Misago hurriedly built a larger chapel that he called the Chapel of Our Lady of Sorrows. However, he did not use Mary's specifications. When people questioned his reasoning, he said, "This is what I can do to welcome the cardinal. Let whoever comes after me do what was supposed to be."

Since my departure from Rwanda in 1998, I had become personally invested in helping to fulfill Mary's mission. After all, Mary used to make the visionaries repeat some messages for the public to hear, and many times, when I was there, she asked them to say, "My children, help me, help me! I am calling you to help me realize my mission." It was a call I took personally, as I knew she was talking to all of us. It was up to us to respond.

When my book *Left to Tell* was published, it put a fire beneath my feet to continue to spread the word about the Marian apparitions and share the miracles of Our Lady with the world. So in 2006, I paid a visit to Rwanda to see if I could speak with the bishop and get him to understand why it was so important to fulfill Mary's wish for two chapels—as she requested them, where she requested them to be built, with the measurements she gave. I believe that just like everywhere else Mary appeared in the world, one of the chapels was meant to be a large basilica.

Additionally, I was curious as to why Bishop Misago had approved only three out of the many visionaries who had received the apparitions, rather than the 11 whom the previous bishop had heartily accepted.

Although he was open to hearing me, he was visibly disturbed. He said, "Just because I didn't accept the other visionaries, I know that doesn't mean they didn't have apparitions. It was actually Segatashya [one of the other visionaries, who had mainly received apparitions of Jesus] who convinced me that the apparitions were happening. I knew he was being truthful because that boy could not make up what he was saying and the theological answers he was giving that have been difficult for seminarists to answer."

I was confused by this admission, as I'd almost expected Bishop Misago to rationalize his decision by saying that he didn't believe all the visionaries had encountered authentic apparitions. "Do you see how confusing this is?" I gently prodded. "Since you didn't approve all of the visionaries, or the apparitions of Jesus, people think you found something wrong in what they said, or that they lied."

He shrugged and replied, "I didn't say they lied or didn't have apparitions. I just had to be careful when it came to approving so-called apparitions of Jesus, which don't happen very often in the world. But it's possible that in the future they will be approved." He went on to say that I wasn't the only person asking him these questions, and he assured me that he would eventually consider building the chapels.

I didn't allow myself to be deterred by the seemingly immovable delay in fulfilling Mary's wishes. Our Lady had always told the visionaries that the way to God was through helping her. She also asked us never to be discouraged or afraid. Our adversaries were like barking dogs; the noises they made may have been frightening, but there was no way they could touch us. I allowed myself to maintain an open and faithful heart.

As I continued to speak with Bishop Misago, I realized that he wasn't simply refusing to build the chapels; he obviously had his reservations, but he wasn't saying no outright. As I continued to press on, he finally admitted, "We don't have an architect for this project. I fear the vision is too beautiful and complicated for anyone to correctly carry it out."

*Well, at least we know the problem now!* I triumphantly thought to myself.

When I was back in the U.S., I spoke to a group of Benedictine priests in Portland, Oregon, and shared with them the vision of Mary's two chapels in Kibeho. I mentioned that the bishop was concerned that the plan was too complex to be fulfilled. One of the priests solemnly proclaimed, "When Our Lady asks for something, you don't argue."

The priest took it upon himself to introduce me to Henry Fitzgibbon, a principal from Soderstrom Architects; the firm had a long history of faith-based projects throughout Oregon. When I told Henry about Our Lady's wishes, I could see the look of determination in his eyes; like me, he wanted to make her vision a reality.

After this, Henry used his own money to travel with me to Rwanda. Together, we met with one of the visionaries, Anathalie, to talk to her about her experience of receiving the vision of Mary's two chapels. We also met with Dr. Muremyangango Bonaventure, a psychiatrist who had originally been hired by the Catholic Church in the 1980s to investigate the veracity of the apparitions. Dr. Bonaventure went into the investigation as an atheist who was convinced that he would be able to debunk the apparitions . . . but he ended up converting to Catholicism and becoming a strong proponent of the visionaries of Kibeho after what he saw. He had seen too many miracles to idly stand by.

As Dr. Bonaventure shared with me, he felt that the young visionaries were spreading a positive message that all of Rwanda needed to hear, as their individual messages of faith focused on the power of love, service, and being the best one could be. Dr. Bonaventure shared that he and his friends' doctors, who were hired to investigate the apparitions, would administer anesthesia to the visionaries 15 minutes before their encounters with Mary, as she often told them in advance when she would be coming to them. While most people would be rendered unconscious under such dosages, the young people would be roused out of unconsciousness as soon as Mary came; they would stand up and receive the apparitions as if nothing had happened. Needles were placed in their eyes, and their skin was burned, but they couldn't feel a thing while they were talking with Mary or Jesus. When Dr. Bonaventure checked their brain activity during the apparitions, all signs indicated that they should have been in a comatose state—but miraculously they were absolutely conscious as they shared their visions of Our Mother. Over time, Dr. Bonaventure certified that the visions were not the cause of mental aberrations or downright fabrications, and he came to promote the apparitions.

When I met Dr. Bonaventure, he was gracious enough to share with me documents from the 1980s, as well as the copious notes he had taken about the apparitions when they occurred. When I introduced Henry to him and told him of our plan to build Mary's chapels (with the approval of Bishop Misago, of course), he was overjoyed. He confided that he felt his plans were fulfilled now that he knew there was an architect up for the task.

Through our conversations with Anathalie and Dr. Bonaventure, as well as our study of the documents the doctor had collected, Henry came up with a beautiful design for Mary's chapels that honored her vision. Henry's basilica was designed to include a number of rooftop structures that would resemble the top of an African peace basket. The design elements melded the illustrious legacy of the Catholic Church and the beauty of Rwandan culture. Hope was resuscitated, and I was inspired to call on Bishop Misago once more.

I went to him on that trip to announce that I had an architect who would bring his passion and expertise to the project, and that I would help to raise the money to fulfill Mary's request. For whatever reason, the bishop had no interest in what I had to say and continued to mete out a variety of excuses for why it could not happen. I sighed to myself, for I understood that his faith had been cut off at the limbs by his own limited thinking. Just a few years later, Bishop Misago passed away from a heart attack, leaving much unfinished business and many unresolved questions among the people of Kibeho, several of whom are still praying that the other visionaries and apparitions of Jesus will someday be approved.

Mary often entreated her children to come to her assistance in order to make her visions a reality on this earth. Mary is always active in our world, and she does not depend on priests or bishops to fulfill her wishes. Historically, she has appeared to simple people who might not have the immediate power to do anything at all. However, Mary has always emphasized that anyone can take her message, and with her guidance disseminate it to the masses in awe-inspiring ways. I knew that it was my responsibility to step up and do what I could.

I was determined to create a foundation so that I could collect the donations of people the world over who had already professed their love and devotion for Mary, as well as their support for realizing her two chapels in Kibeho. After all, Kibeho was a large and active center for Catholics and those who loved Mary, regardless of their religious affiliation. Thousands of people came to this holy place to pay their respects, so I was well aware that there would be widespread support for our mission.

## THE UNEXPECTED AID OF POPE FRANCIS

Remarkably, I would find an ally right at the center of the Vatican.

In October 2014, I had the pleasure of meeting the Bravos, a beautiful family from Argentina, whose son, Angelo, was a polo player who had recently died of brain cancer. The Bravos had contacted me for a very specific purpose. Not long before, they were in Rome and had received the chance to meet with Pope Francis. At that time, Angelo's tumor had progressed to the point that he could not speak, but the pope gently said, "Do not worry, my son. If you read this wonderful book, you'll see that the woman who wrote it spoke a great deal . . . even in times when she could not utter a single word with her mouth. You can still speak in your mind and spirit. Speak to God and he will answer you."

By God's grace, the book that Pope Francis had recommended was my book, *Left to Tell*, which chronicled the story of how I survived the Rwandan genocide through my faith in God. As the Bravos later told me, they purchased the book, and along with Angelo's dear wife, Ruth, they would read it to their dying son. Every time they stopped after reading a few pages, Angelo would push their hands to indicate that he wanted them to continue. Tears rolled down my face as they shared that they'd read the book to him within a week of his death, and they were assured that Angelo died in peace because of my book.

His family vowed that they would find a way to ensure that I, too, could meet Pope Francis; their good friend, Father Jorge, arranged a meeting. Jorge would accompany me and translate from English to Spanish for Pope Francis.

I was ecstatic. A few years earlier, I had met Pope Benedict when I was invited to speak in Rome—I was so happy, and it was the kind of happiness that paralyzed me so completely that I forgot everything I'd planned to say . . . except for my request that the Holy Father bless me and my rosary. This time around, I was similarly honored to meet Pope Francis. I knew that our meeting would be no more than three to four minutes. I was determined that whatever I would share this time would be more "important" than what I'd shared with the previous pope. You don't go all the way to Rome to say "hi" to the pope!

While in Rome, the day before I met Pope Francis, something strange happened. I was reading a book in my hotel about a famous basilica in Rome, known as Our Lady of the Snows, or St. Mary Major Basilica, which is the only church that was built to Mary's exact measurements and requirements. This church was raised in the 4th century by Pope Liberius, and it was rebuilt by Pope Sixtus III after the Council of Ephesus proclaimed Mary as the Mother of God, in 431. At that time, the basilica was officially rededicated to Our Mother.

The church is also known as Our Lady of the Snows, and there is a beautiful story behind how it came to be. One legend notes that a Roman nobleman named Giovanni and his wife were without children. They prayed to the Virgin Mary for an heir; they vowed that if they received an answer to their prayers, they would build a church in her honor. They had a spontaneous vision of Mary in which she professed her wish for a church to be built in honor of her on the Esquiline Hill, one of the seven great hills of Rome. She noted that the exact measurements and layout of the church would be verified because they would soon be outlined in snow. Giovanni and his wife were dumbfounded, for it was August! How was this possible?

Giovanni was a close friend of Pope Liberius, so he approached him. The pope was curious about this visitation, so he prayed for a visitation from Mary to ensure that it was really her wish to have a church built. Amazingly, the Pope soon had a dream in which Mary confirmed that it was indeed so; in fact, Mary said that she would show them the exact place very soon. Giovanni and the pope had little reason to doubt or question Mary, for on August 5, in the year 352, snow fell on the Esquiline Hill in the midst of a heat wave. The outline of what would be Mary's basilica was quickly recorded, and Pope Liberius commenced with the building of the Basilica of Our Lady of the Snows. Currently, it is the largest church in the world dedicated to Mary. It is a gorgeous early Roman basilica full of mosaics that attest to its magnificent history.

When I read the story, I asked the people at the front desk of my hotel if they knew about the church. I was shocked to discover that it was within walking distance! I immediately walked to the basilica, amazed that I had never heard about it before that day— and awed that, by providence, I was staying so close to it! However, it didn't surprise me, as I'd encountered similar miracles in the past. I saw the hand of Mary herself in this matter. I could feel that she saw my eagerness to help fulfill her plans, and she was aiding me in doing so. My heart filled with the grace of God that day, as I sat in the basilica. My previous doubts were completely quelled as I gave in to the peace and majesty of this beautiful, sacred place, where so many people had been embraced by Mary's unfaltering love for humanity. I knew that Mary was bolstering my faith, reminding me that I'd come here for a reason; and brief or not, my meeting with the pope hadn't come out of nowhere—it was a Godsent privilege. I had been sent by Mary, and all the connections I'd made that led me to that moment had not arrived out of nowhere; they'd been made for a reason. I didn't want to offend the pope or put him in a difficult position, nor did I want to upset any of the church officials in Kibeho! However, the truth overrode those concerns, and I realized that my personal feelings could not come before God's plans.

I had already rehearsed what I would share with the pope, which would be even briefer than the three or four minutes I'd been afforded, considering that Father Jorge was tasked with translating my words into Spanish. I knew that I wanted to reiterate all the things that Mary had asked Rwandans to do—including praying the Seven Sorrows Rosary and creating prayer groups—and that because we had not heeded her instructions and warnings, the genocide had occurred. I wanted the pope to understand that we had yet to fulfill Mary's wish that two chapels with specific measurements be built to honor her apparitions in Kibeho. Given the dire state of the world, the unwillingness to obey Our Mother could only lead to needless suffering. As one of the world's great humanitarians, the pope would surely understand the urgency and necessity of the chapel project in Kibeho. This is why I had to ask him to support us. I knew it was a bold request, but the Vatican had already approved the apparitions in Kibeho, so I felt we were honor bound to realize Mary's plan at last.

I realized the pope wouldn't have the time to figure out how to support this tiny country in Africa, so I decided that I would make a suggestion: "If you ask them, I know they will fulfill Mary's request." I was also aware that he might politely listen but do nothing about it. Still, Mary's inspiration rang like a clear bell in my heart. Even if the pope didn't listen to me, he would heed Mary. I was only a link in the long chain of making her requests come true.

I finalized my plan with Father Jorge, and when the time came for the meeting, I poured my heart out to the pope, being sure to mention the history of the apparitions in Kibeho, as well as Mary's request that two chapels be built for her. I will never forget the pope's response as he listened to Jorge's translation of my passionate plea. He gently placed his hand on mine, looked into my eyes, and said that he would make the call to the Diocese of Gikongoro. At the time, I was honored that this very busy man would make such a promise to me, but a part of me doubted that he would follow through. I did not doubt his sincerity, but given the sheer number of people he meets on a daily basis, I was convinced that he would quickly forget.

However, miracles have a way of following the devoted. Afterward, a woman who had been present during our meeting, as she was someone who was quite close to the pope, quickly came running after me. "Excuse me! What did you just say to the pope? I would like to know, because he listened so intently and said that he would do what you asked."

It turned out this woman was a journalist in Rome, so I sat down and told her a bit about my request to the pope, as well as the eight long years of attempting to convince church officials in Kibeho to build Mary's two chapels. I explained that I had already secured an architect for the project and had the capacity to raise the money for it, but that the bishop's resistance had long been a roadblock. After listening to my story, the journalist said that she'd write it all down and ensure that Pope Francis would receive this document so he could read it the following Monday. In this way, my request would hopefully be imprinted in his memory so that he would be inspired to do something about it. I thanked her for her kindness, but I thought little of the meeting . . . until two weeks later, when something remarkable happened: the pope had appointed a new bishop of the Diocese of Gikongoro, of which Kibeho is a part!

After Bishop Misago's death in 2012, there was an interim bishop of Gikongoro, but the role had remained unoccupied for more than two years. However, as the Bravo family informed me, the pope had called Rwanda only to discover that there was no bishop of Gikongoro. He immediately saw to it that a new bishop was appointed: Father Célestin Hakizimana. The pope was also quick to tell the new bishop, "I want the chapels that Our Lady requested to be built."

Whenever a new bishop offers their first mass, they share their primary goals for their station. Before a crowd of 20,000 people, Bishop Célestin said, "My number-one goal is to build the chapels for Our Lady that she requested so many years ago." My heart soared at the news, as it confirmed what my friends had told me. The Vatican was on Mary's side!

### The Faith to See the Project Through

Shortly after his appointment, I went to see the new bishop, who had called me to discuss building Mary's chapels. Both of us were excited about the undertaking, and it was beautiful to see how committed he was to creating a new basilica that would welcome pilgrims from around the world. Finally, I thought, we would be getting down to business!

Unfortunately, the challenge of answering Our Mother's request was not over just yet. Within a year of our meeting, the bishop began to express reservations. Apparently, one very vocal priest in the diocese was very much against the project and took every opportunity to convey his disapproval. In one meeting he proposed the bishop build the chapels on another hill that was different from the place Mary chose. When I insisted that it was the Mother of God who had made the request for a specific placement, he angrily replied, "Mary listens to the bishops, and they have the last word." Another priest said, "We will build where we want, as Mary is surely not coming to build them herself." I was shocked by this, as it felt like sacrilege to me, but nobody contradicted these ideas; in fact, they seemed to have the effect of sowing doubt among the other priests.

Still, Bishop Célestin did not say that he was against the building of the chapels. I knew that he was a good man, and in fact, he had saved the lives of hundreds of Tutsis who'd taken refuge at St. Paul Church in downtown Kigali during the genocide. Although I believed he was misguided, I knew he would eventually come to his senses and make the right decision. Years later, the priest who had spoken out against the building of the chapels left the Church altogether. Bishop Célestin then approached Henry and me to ask if we'd be able to find a different location to build Mary's chapels.

Given Our Mother's request for the exact location of the chapels, I was both angry and reluctant. Henry and I were willing to explore other possibilities out of respect for the bishop, but inside I thought that if they were to proceed to build somewhere other than where Mary had specified, I would just stop getting involved.

Ultimately, we came back to the bishop. Henry explained to him, "We can put the chapels anywhere you wish, your excellency—in a valley or on a mountain. Anything is possible, but you should know that the construction will cost you three or four times more if you were to build it anywhere other than the place where Mary asked for it to be built. Our Mother is all-knowing, and she understood that the location in Kibeho was the most reasonable and cost-effective place for the basilica."

Although Bishop Célestin was open to this possibility, he came to us with a new request: "Why don't we just put it where Kibeho High School is?" While I objected, Henry was willing to explore this possibility.

Kibeho High School was located right next to the area where the apparitions had occurred, but building a basilica in its place would destroy the school, an important part of the history of the Marian apparitions. The nuns who ran the school came to Henry and me in tears, as they were shaken by the possibility that the school might be removed altogether.

At this time, I was also in contact with Anathalie, the visionary who had walked the grounds to indicate where Mary wanted her chapels to be built. I was surprised and disappointed that Anathalie now seemed to be against the establishment of the two chapels. "This issue seems to be causing so much trouble," she said. "Perhaps we should just listen to the priests and put it somewhere else. Let's not disturb the current site."

I asked Anathalie if Mary had asked her to change her mind; she replied, "No, but she will understand."

I thought back to Dr. Bonaventure's investigation of the apparitions in the 1980s. I remembered that Mary had once told Anathalie, "Blessed are those who will not confuse your words with mine." I realized that the visionaries are only human at the end of the day. While I believed in the integrity of their visions, I also understood that Mary had never intended for people to simply succumb to the visionaries' personal interpretations of her words.

To think that a piece of information from 1983 could come to assist me in 2020! One of the other original visionaries, Alphonsine, who is now a nun in Italy, affirmed my feelings. She told me, "Each of us must pray for our own understanding of what Mary told the visionaries. If you believe you are doing what is written, don't worry about what Anathalie or I have to say."

Thankfully, after his own conversations with some people who were present during Anathalie's apparition of Mary offering the specifications for the chapel, Bishop Célestin finally decided that he would not raze Kibeho High School; he would approve the building of the two chapels, which meant that I could finally begin collecting the necessary funds through a foundation that would support the $45 million project. At first, the bishop was resistant to the plan, as he wanted to exert full control over the project, even though I explained to him that we had to be accountable to the individuals, organizations, and governments who would be giving us the funds. I assured him that I would not be making a single penny off the enterprise—only the architects and builders would be paid for their work. I was simply the middlewoman, there to ensure that Mary's wishes would be properly fulfilled.

Because Bishop Célestin was resistant, we eventually went to the cardinal Antoine Kambanda for advice, since he was a higher authority. The mayor of the Nyaruguru District of which Kibeho was a part, Francois Habitegeko, got wind of the situation and suggested that we meet with Bishop Célestin to come up with a plan that would work for everyone. The bishop conceded. A committee was formed to ensure that the project would have proper oversight, to ensure that all donations would be managed with the utmost respect and integrity.

As I write this book, I am preparing to visit Rwanda weeks from now to finalize the plans for breaking ground in Kibeho. I am overjoyed that after 16 years of work, and the dedication of so many devout people, there is a light at the end of the tunnel.

I have learned throughout all of this that the people who love Our Mother may be quiet and humble, but they are willing to give anything and everything to honor and support her vision for humanity—and they number many in all corners of the world. My wish is that the chapels will be erected by 2025 for a grand opening that will draw devotees from all corners of the world. I have been praying for this every day for the last several years, and the obstacles have only made my faith and determination stronger. Anything is possible when it comes to Our Mother!

I hope my words will convince some of you to make the special pilgrimage to Kibeho, a place abundant with miracles. Perhaps when you do, the two chapels Our Lady requested will have finally been built, and they will greet you atop the hill like the castle of God I envisioned when I was a young girl.

Mary promised that Kibeho would be visited by millions of people from every corner of the world, and that those who sought her comfort and love would be heartened, and their faith made even stronger. She is there now, waiting, calling to the world to come to her to receive blessings beyond imagination. Who can refuse her when she calls? She may be Our Lady of Kibeho, Mother of the Word, and Our Lady of Sorrows—but she is also the Blessed Mother of the entire world.

# PART II

# CONTEMPLATING

## THE

# SEVEN SORROWS

CHAPTER 4

# THE SEVEN SORROWS

## AS A

# SPIRITUAL PRACTICE

Mary's presence is one unified gift of love that is both natural and supernatural, in that she loved Jesus as both her son and her God. Those who have the greatest capacity for love also have the greatest capacity for sorrow and suffering, which is why Mary was revered among the great martyrs.

The Seven Sorrows, as well as the Seven Promises offered by the grace of Our Lady, are meant to show us that our suffering, our sacrifices, and our losses have meaning when we offer them to her and to God. So often, people seek out worldly riches, passing pleasure, and a comfort that keeps their hearts safe and closed. But through the gift of the Seven Sorrows, we can see that the more we try to avoid pain in search of pleasure, the greater the disappointments and suffering that will eventually come to pass.

An angel once told St. Bridget that Our Mother was so bountiful in her mercy that she was willing to suffer any pain rather than witness unredeemed souls who encountered suffering themselves. The angel went on to say that Mary found consolation amid her own sorrow at the death of her beloved son, in that she prayed that the world would be redeemed by his death and that all sinners would be reconciled with God.

The Holy Virgin promised that when prayed with an open and repentant heart, the rosary would win us the Lord's forgiveness for our sins and free our souls from guilt and remorse. She also promised that over time, the rosary would develop within us a deep understanding of why we sin, and that knowledge would give us the wisdom and strength to change or remove any internal flaws, weaknesses of character, or personality traits causing unhappiness and keeping us from enjoying the lives God intended for us.

Below are the Seven Sorrows and the Seven Promises of Mary, as revealed by Our Blessed Mother to St. Bridget of Sweden in the 14th century, and then again to Marie-Claire of Kibeho, Rwanda, in the 20th century, and as they can be used in prayer. This chapter offers some insight into the ritual of working with the Seven Sorrows Rosary as it was introduced to us by the visionary Marie-Claire.

## THE ROSARY OF THE SEVEN SORROWS

This rosary recalls the Seven Sorrows that the Virgin Mary suffered through—albeit with love and compassion—during the life, trials, and agonizing death of her son, Jesus Christ. It's very special to the immaculate heart of the Blessed Mother, and she wants all of us to say it as often as possible.

The Rosary of the Seven Sorrows contains all the power you need to change your life for the better, obtain peace and happiness, realize your true potential, fulfill all your dreams, and grow closer to God's light. During one of her many apparitions to Marie-Claire, the Holy Virgin suggested that it be prayed every day, but especially on Tuesdays and Fridays: Tuesday being the day Mary first appeared to Marie-Claire, and Friday being the day Jesus was crucified.

The Blessed Mother also stressed that the Rosary of the Seven Sorrows is intended to complement—and in no way replace—the traditional rosary. Pray both rosaries regularly and you'll be doubly blessed!

The following is a description of this amazing rosary as the Virgin Mary herself taught it to Marie-Claire in Kibeho. It may be prayed aloud or contemplated silently, alone or with others; the key is for the prayers, reflections, and meditations to always come from the depths of your heart as you vividly consider what Mary must have felt as she was undergoing these ordeals.

I speak from experience when I promise that you'll never regret learning this wonderful rosary and that you'll soon lose track of the countless blessings that praying it will bring into your life. It's my hope that more people than ever before will learn just how amazing this rosary is. If you don't have the rosary beads, just follow the diagram and instructions on page 50. (It is, however, important that when you reach each sorrowful mystery, you take a moment to meditate on the magnitude of Mary's suffering . . . and the strength of her love.)

## INTRODUCTORY PRAYERS

Begin with the following prayer:

*My God, I offer you this rosary for your glory, so I may honor your Holy Mother, the Blessed Virgin, so I can share and meditate upon her suffering. I humbly beg you to give me true repentance for all my sins. Give me wisdom and humility so that I may receive all the indulgences contained in this prayer.*

Follow this with an act of contrition:

*O my God, I am heartily sorry for having offended you, and I detest all my sins because I dread the loss of heaven and the pains of hell; but most of all because they offend you, my*

# How to Pray
## the Rosary of the Seven Sorrows

1. On the large medal at the bottom of the rosary:
   a. Make the sign of the cross.
   b. Say the Introductory Prayer.
   c. Say the Act of Contrition.

2. For each of the next three beads, say a Hail Mary.

3. On the first small medal:
   a. Say the prayer, "Most merciful mother, remind us always about the sorrows of your son, Jesus."
   b. Meditate upon the First Sorrowful Mystery.
   c. Say the Lord's Prayer.

4. For each of the next seven beads, say a Hail Mary.

5. On the second small medal:
   a. Say the prayer, "Most merciful mother . . . "
   b. Meditate upon the Second Sorrowful Mystery.
   c. Say the Lord's Prayer.

6. For each of the next seven beads, say a Hail Mary.

7. On the third small medal:
   a. Say the prayer, "Most merciful mother . . . "
   b. Meditate upon the Third Sorrowful Mystery.
   c. Say the Lord's Prayer.

8. For each of the next seven beads, say a Hail Mary.

9. On the fourth small medal:
   a. Say the prayer, "Most merciful mother . . . "
   b. Meditate upon the Fourth Sorrowful Mystery.
   c. Say the Lord's Prayer.

10. For each of the next seven beads, say a Hail Mary.

11. On the fifth small medal:
    a. Say the prayer, "Most merciful mother . . . "
    b. Meditate upon the Fifth Sorrowful Mystery.
    c. Say the Lord's Prayer.

12. For each of the next seven beads, say a Hail Mary.

13. On the sixth small medal:
    a. Say the prayer, "Most merciful mother . . . "
    b. Meditate upon the Sixth Sorrowful Mystery.
    c. Say the Lord's Prayer.

14. For each of the next seven beads, say a Hail Mary.

15. On the seventh small medal:
    a. Say the prayer, "Most merciful mother . . . "
    b. Meditate upon the Seventh Sorrowful Mystery.
    c. Say the Lord's Prayer.

16. For each of the next seven beads, say a Hail Mary.

17. Upon reaching the large medal at the bottom of the rosary:
    a. Say the prayer, "Most merciful mother . . . "
    b. Say the Concluding Prayer.
    c. Say three times: "Mary, who was conceived without sin and who suffered for us, pray for us."

Make a sign of the cross; your prayers will be answered!

*God, you who are all good and deserving of all my love. I firmly resolve, with the help of your grace, to confess my sins, to do penance, and to amend my life. Amen.*

Followed by: *Three Hail Marys*

Before each sorrow, pray:

*Most merciful Mother, remind us always about the sorrows of your son, Jesus.*

## The First Sorrow

*The Prophecy of Simeon* (Luke 2:22–35): The Blessed Virgin Mary took Jesus to the temple, as tradition demanded that all newborns be blessed in the temple before God. There, the old priest Simeon held the baby Jesus in his hands, and the Holy Spirit filled his heart. Simeon recognized Jesus as the promised Savior and held the child high toward heaven, thanking God for granting his wish that he would live long enough to behold the Messiah. "Now your servant may depart this life in peace, my Lord," he said. Then he looked upon Mary and proclaimed, "And you, woman, a sword of sorrow will pierce your heart because of the suffering that shall befall your child."

The Blessed Virgin knew that she had given birth to the Savior of humankind, so she immediately understood and accepted Simeon's prophecy. Although her heart was deeply touched by this favor of bearing the baby Jesus, her heart remained heavy and troubled, for she knew what had been written about the ordeals and subsequent death of the Savior. Whenever she saw her son, she was constantly reminded of the suffering he would be subjected to, and his suffering became her own.

**Prayer:**

*Beloved Mother Mary, whose heart suffered beyond bearing because of us, teach us to suffer with you and with love, and to accept all the suffering God deems it necessary to send our way. Let us suffer, and may our suffering be known to God only, like yours and that of Jesus. Do not let us show our suffering to the world, so it will matter more and be used to atone for the sins of the world. You, Mother, who suffered with the Savior of the world, we offer you our suffering, and the suffering of the world, because we are your children. Join those sorrows to your own and to those of the Lord Jesus Christ, then offer them to God the Father so that he will know the one who created it. You are a mother greater than all.*

Followed by: *Our Father and seven Hail Marys*

## The Second Sorrow

*The Flight into Egypt* (Matthew 2:13–15): Mary's heart broke and her mind was greatly troubled when Joseph revealed to her the words of the angel. They were to wake up quickly and flee to Egypt because Herod wanted to kill Jesus. The Blessed Virgin hardly had time to decide what to take or leave behind; she took her child and left everything else, rushing outside before Joseph so that they could hurry as God wished. Then she said, "Even though God has power over everything, he wants us to flee with Jesus, his son. God will show us the way, and we shall arrive without being caught by the enemy."

Because the Blessed Virgin was the mother of Jesus, she loved him more than anyone else. Her heart was deeply troubled at the sight of her infant son's discomfort, and she suffered greatly because he was cold and shivering. While she and her husband were tired, sleepy, and hungry during this long travel, Mary's only thought was about the safety and comfort of her child. She feared coming face-to-face with the soldiers who had been ordered to kill Jesus because she was aware that the enemy was still in Bethlehem.

Her heart remained constantly anguished during this flight. She also knew that where they were going, there would be no friendly faces to greet them.

**Prayer:**

> *Beloved Mother, who has suffered so much, give to us your courageous heart. Give us strength so that we can be brave like you and accept with love the suffering God sends our way. Help us to also accept all the suffering we inflict upon ourselves and the suffering inflicted upon us by others. Heavenly Mother, you alone purify our suffering so that we may give glory to God and save our souls.*

Followed by: *Our Father and seven Hail Marys*

## The Third Sorrow

*The Loss of Jesus in the Temple* (Luke 2:41–52): Jesus was the only begotten Son of God, but he was also Mary's child. The Blessed Virgin loved Jesus more than herself because he was her God. Compared to other children, he was most unique because he was already living as God. When Mary lost Jesus on their way back from Jerusalem, the world became so big and lonely that she believed she couldn't go on living without him, so great was her sorrow. (She felt the same pain her son felt when he was later abandoned by his apostles during the Passion.)

As the Holy Mother looked anxiously for her beloved boy, deep pain welled in her heart. She blamed herself, asking why she didn't take greater care of him. But it was not her fault; Jesus no longer needed her protection as before. What really hurt Mary was that her son had decided to stay behind without her consent. Jesus had pleased her in everything so far; he never annoyed her in any way, nor would he ever displease his parents. She knew that he always did what was necessary, however, so she never suspected him of being disobedient.

**Prayer:**

*Beloved Mother, teach us to accept all our sufferings because of our sins and to atone for the sins of the whole world.*

Followed by: *Our Father and seven Hail Marys*

## The Fourth Sorrow

*Mary Meets Jesus on the Way to Calvary* (Luke 23:27–31): Mary witnessed Jesus carrying the heavy cross alone—the cross on which he was to be crucified. This didn't surprise the Blessed Virgin because she already knew about the approaching death of Our Lord. Noting how her son was already weakened by the numerous hard blows given by the soldiers' clubs, she was filled with anguish at his pain.

The soldiers kept hurrying and pushing him, though he had no strength left. He fell, exhausted, unable to raise himself. At that moment, Mary's eyes, so full of tender love and compassion, met her son's eyes, which were pained and covered in blood. Their hearts seemed to be sharing the load; every pain he felt, she felt as well. They knew that nothing could be done except to believe and trust in God and dedicate their suffering to him. All they could do was put everything in God's hands.

**Prayer:**

*Beloved Mother, so stricken with grief, help us to bear our own suffering with courage and love so that we may relieve your sorrowful heart and that of Jesus. In doing so, may we give glory to God who gave you and Jesus to humanity. As you suffered, teach us to suffer silently and patiently. Grant unto us the grace of loving God in everything. O Mother of Sorrows, most afflicted of all mothers, have mercy on the sinners of the whole world.*

Followed by: *Our Father and seven Hail Marys*

## The Fifth Sorrow

*Mary Stands at the Foot of the Cross* (John 19:25–27): The Blessed
Virgin Mary continued to climb the mount to Calvary, following
behind Jesus painfully and sorrowfully, yet suffering silently. She
could see him staggering and falling with the cross some more,
and she witnessed her son being beaten by soldiers who pulled his
hair to force him to stand up. Despite his innocence, when Jesus
reached the top of Calvary, he was ordered to confess in front of
the crowd so they could laugh at him. Mary deeply felt her son's
pain and humiliation, particularly when his tormentors forced
him to strip off what was left of his clothing. The Blessed Virgin
felt sick at heart seeing these tyrants crucifying her son naked,
shaming him terribly merely to amuse the jeering crowd. (Jesus
and Mary felt more disgrace than normal people did because they
were holy and without sin.)

The Blessed Virgin Mary felt pain beyond bearing when Jesus
was stretched out on the cross. His murderers sang merrily as they
approached him with hammers and nails. They sat on him heavily so that he could not move when they spiked him to the wood.
As they hammered the nails through his hands and feet, Mary
felt the blows in her heart; the nails pierced her flesh as they tore
into her son's body. She felt her life fading away. As the soldiers
lifted the cross to drop it into the hole they'd dug, they deliber-
ately jerked it, causing the force of Jesus's bodily weight to tear
through the flesh on his hands and expose his bone. The pain
shot through his body like liquid fire. He endured three excruciating hours skewered on the cross, yet the physical pain was nothing compared to the agonizing heartache he was forced to bear
seeing his mother suffering below him. Mercifully, he finally died.

### Prayer:

*Beloved Mother, Queen of the Martyrs, give us the cour-
age you had in all your sufferings so that we may unite our
sufferings with yours and give glory to God. Help us follow*

*all his commandments and those of the Church so that Our Lord's sacrifice will not be in vain, and all sinners in the world will be saved.*

Followed by: *Our Father and seven Hail Marys*

## The Sixth Sorrow

*Mary Receives the Dead Body of Jesus in Her Arms* (John 19:38–40): The friends of Jesus, Joseph and Nicodemus, took down his body from the cross and placed it in the outstretched arms of the Blessed Virgin. Then Mary washed it with deep respect and love because she was his mother. She knew better than anyone else that he was God incarnate who'd taken a human body to become the Savior of all people. Mary could see the terrifying wounds from the flogging Jesus had received while at Pilate's. His flesh had been shredded, and large strips had been torn from his back. His entire body had been so lacerated that gaping wounds crisscrossed him from head to toe. Mary found that the wounds from the nails were less severe than those caused by the flogging and by carrying the cross. She was horrified at the thought that her son had managed to carry the heavy, splintered cross all the way to Calvary. She saw the circle of blood the crown of thorns had made on his forehead and, to her horror, realized that many of the barbed thorns had dug so deeply into his skull they had penetrated his brain.

Looking at her broken boy, the Holy Mother knew that his agonizing death was far worse than the torture reserved for the wickedest of criminals. As she cleaned his damaged body, she envisioned him during each stage of his short life, remembering her first look at his beautiful newborn face as the two of them lay in the manger, and every day in between, until this heartrending moment as she gently bathed his lifeless body. Her anguish was relentless as she prepared her son and Lord for burial, but she remained brave and strong, becoming the true Queen of Martyrs. As she washed her son, she prayed that everybody would know the riches of paradise and enter the gates of heaven. She prayed for every soul in the world to embrace God's love so her son's torturous death would benefit all humankind and would not have been in vain. Mary prayed for the world; she prayed for all of us.

**Prayer:**

*We thank you, Beloved Mother, for your courage as you stood beneath your dying child to comfort him on the cross. As our Savior drew his last breath, you became a wonderful mother to all of us; you became the Blessed Mother of the world. We know that you love us more than our own earthly parents do. We implore you to be our advocate before the throne of mercy and grace so that we can truly become your children. We thank you for Jesus, our Savior and Redeemer, and we thank Jesus for giving you to us. Please pray for us, Mother.*

Followed by: *Our Father and seven Hail Marys*

## The Seventh Sorrow

*Jesus Is Placed in the Tomb* (John 19:41–42): The life of the Blessed Virgin Mary was so closely linked to that of Jesus, she thought there was no reason for her to go on living any longer. Her only comfort was that his death had ended his unspeakable suffering. Our Sorrowful Mother, with the help of John and the holy women, devoutly placed Jesus's body in the sepulchre, and she left him there as any other dead person. She went home with great pain and tremendous sorrow; for the first time she was without him, and her loneliness was a new and bitter source of pain. Her heart had been dying since her son's heart had stopped beating, but she was certain that our Savior would soon be resurrected.

**Prayer:**

*Most Beloved Mother, whose beauty surpassed that of all mothers, Mother of Mercy, Mother of Jesus, and Mother to us all, we are your children and we place all our trust in you. Teach us to see God in all things and all situations, even in our sufferings. Help us to understand the importance of suffering, and also to know the purpose of our suffering as God had intended it. You yourself were conceived and born without sin, were preserved from sin, yet you suffered more than anybody else has. You accepted suffering and pain with love and with unsurpassed courage. You stood by your son from the time he was arrested until he died. You suffered along with him, felt every pain and torment he did. You accomplished the will of God the Father; and according to his will, you have become our savior with Jesus. We beg you, dear Mother, to teach us to do as Jesus did. Teach us to accept our cross courageously. We trust you, most Merciful Mother, so teach us to sacrifice for all the sinners in the world. Help us to follow in your son's footsteps, and even to be willing to lay down our lives for others.*

### Concluding Prayer

Say:

*Queen of Martyrs, your heart suffered so much. I beg you, by the merits of the tears you shed in these terrible and sorrowful times, to obtain for me and all the sinners of the world the grace of complete sincerity and repentance. Amen.*

Three times, say: *Mary, who conceived without sin and who suffered for us, pray for us.*

Congratulations on finishing the Rosary of the Seven Sorrows of the Virgin Mary! Now make the sign of the cross to wipe away the tears Mary shed during the Passion of Jesus, and rest assured that your prayers will be answered!

## THE SEVEN PROMISES

Rejoice in the Seven Promises offered by Our Mother, as revealed by St. Bridget and Marie-Claire, to all her children who faithfully observe her Seven Sorrows:

1.  I will grant peace to their families.
2.  They will be enlightened about the divine mysteries.
3.  I will console them in their pains, and I will accompany them in their work.
4.  I will give them as much as they ask for as long as it does not oppose the adorable will of my Divine Son or the sanctification of their souls.
5.  I will defend them in their spiritual battles with the infernal enemy, and I will protect them at every instant of their lives.
6.  I will visibly help them at the moment of their death; they will see the face of their Mother.
7.  I have obtained from my Divine Son that those who propagate this devotion to my tears and dolors will be taken directly from this earthly life to eternal happiness, since all their sins will be forgiven and my son and I will be their eternal consolation and joy.

We were also given four Principle Graces, or promises to the devotees of Our Mother's Seven Sorrows (as revealed to St. Elizabeth, from the book *The Glories of Mary* by St. Alphonsus Liguori):

1.  That those who before death invoke the Divine Mother in the name of her sorrows will obtain true repentance of all their sins
2.  That he will protect all who have this devotion in their tribulations, and will protect them especially at the hour of death

3. That he will impress on their minds the remembrance of his Passion

4. That he will place such devout servants in Mother Mary's hands to do with them as she wishes and to obtain for them all the graces she desires

## HOW TO INTEGRATE THE SEVEN SORROWS ROSARY INTO YOUR LIFE

The Blessed Virgin gave the Seven Sorrows to St. Bridget so many centuries ago, but understandably, many aspects of the prayer were changed over time and many people have also forgotten it, which is why Mary reappeared to Marie-Claire—to clear out the dogma and offer a simple, accessible format for leading people through the prayer. She also wanted to remind people that the Seven Sorrows Rosary is a gift that is especially pertinent to people in this moment we live in now.

Aside from that, this rosary is a powerful method for helping people to bring their feelings to the surface. Mary reveals her genius and understanding as the Mother of us all, as she encouraged the visionaries to pay close attention to their feelings rather than attempting to censor or deny them. She shares the depths of her own pain with them and gives them a secure model to follow as they deal with their own.

So often, we are conditioned to pray in an impersonal way that does not necessarily bring forth the sincerity that is required to share ourselves fully with Our Lord. There have been times when I was reluctant to allow my own sorrow and tears to rise up from the depths and come to the surface. But Mary gently requests that we consider our own pain and specific experiences of feeling hopeless or defeated. She also asks that we put ourselves in her shoes, to experience the power of empathy and our beautiful human capacity to feel deeply for another person's suffering. For when we open our hearts and feel our pain, we can heal and understand what others are feeling. But when we close our hearts to our pain, we also close them to love.

Every single one of us can use the Seven Sorrows Rosary to reenter the places where we remain heartbroken, where we might have been plunged into discomfort, death, and destruction that lay waste to our lives, or where we have been traumatized by others— as in the case of war or genocide, which too many people across our world have experienced. I am still surprised at how much pain I hold in my heart when I stop to reflect on it. For example, I think back to the experience of collecting the remains of my deceased family members after the genocide in Rwanda. Words cannot describe the anguish I felt as one of only two remaining members of my beloved family; I had survived the genocide, but I didn't know how I would survive being alone, or how I would survive in the aftermath of my family's suffering.

Over time, I healed from the loss and was able to function in my life, but there was still a wound in my heart that I didn't want to stop to think about. When I pray the rosary, I experience the presence of this wound, but I also experience the healing balm that Mary brings. When I open myself up to that pain, the Blessed Virgin reminds me that not only am I capable of bearing it, but she is also by my side, offering consolation and succor in the way that a mother would.

Our Lady was always very clear that the Seven Sorrows Rosary was a gift for the entire world. I believe this is the case because she understood that every single one of us experiences pain and suffering. The sad thing is, so many of us either push it down and numb ourselves to our reality, while others use their pain as an excuse to inflict it on others or to act in vengeful ways. The rosary is a profound way to learn to bear our suffering, and to let it open us up to greater love rather than hate and rancor. It gives us a way to alchemize our pain instead of stuffing it down or hiding it, because when our hearts break open in this way, we get to experience the gifts of salvation and love that Mary and Jesus always intended for us to have.

Our Lady also noted that the graces and promises that she would offer were for those who would not only say the prayer but also open their hearts to deeply *feeling* it, allowing the words to resonate on the level of their emotions and thoughts. My advice as you incorporate the rosary into your life is to make sure that you don't go through it too quickly. Don't be mechanical or perfunctory with it. Give yourself time to linger on each of the mysteries. Ask yourself: "What would I feel if this had been me? What would I have done if I were in Mary's shoes?" Picture yourself there, with Mary and Jesus, feeling for them, consoling them. If you cry, that's perfectly fine. You are giving love to the ones who have always loved you so much, and in doing so you are becoming receptive to their power and support.

The more you do this, the more you will find yourself modeling your life after both Mary and Jesus. You will find yourself not wallowing in the suffering or attempting to avoid it but allowing it into your life with dignity and compassion. You will experience God's love for you.

Mary told Marie-Claire that the Seven Sorrows Rosary is similar to a wreath. If you say it every day, you become part of the wreath, entwined with Jesus and Mary as you consider their lives, but also your own. The grace that flows through them will also flow through you. You will feel their blessings, as well as their protection.

This is an especially powerful prayer when it comes to helping people deal with trauma and accept pain as a part of everyday life; when we open their hearts, the rosary shows us that healing and salvation is possible. Mary reminds us that it is perfectly okay to feel our pain, but we need never be alone in the midst of it. We can cry cleansing tears that accompany our confessions and heartfelt sharing with Mary. We don't need to wait until things are too heavy. This can be one way of developing a relationship with Mary in which we feel the presence of our loving Mother and also of building resilience and spiritual strength. We will also see the areas where we have wronged God and failed to love ourselves and others, and we will have the strength to overcome our mistakes.

The next several chapters will offer some further complements to this process of working with the Seven Sorrows Rosary; they will include in-depth ways to contemplate each of the Seven Sorrows and integrate their lessons into your life in a practical way. I have also woven my own story of suffering, loss, and transformation throughout the chapters, to offer a real-life example of what it means to pray the Seven Sorrows in the context of one's own life. At the end of each chapter is an additional prayer for that particular sorrow, as well as some reflection questions that I invite you to ask yourself, through either contemplation or journaling.

I highly recommend creating a sacred space for yourself as you connect with the Seven Sorrows Rosary and incorporate it into your life. For myself, I enjoy having a space in my home where I have room for a Bible, a cross, a statue of Mary, rosary beads, spiritual books, some beautiful flowers, and a candle. With just these implements, my space becomes a sanctuary where I can intimately share with my Mother what is happening in my life. I do my best to slow down, be with my feelings, talk to God and Mary, and remember that I am never alone. Our Father and the Blessed Virgin are always with me, just as they are always with you.

# CHAPTER 5

# THE FIRST SORROW

## The Prophecy of Simeon

*And Simeon blessed them, and said to Mary his mother: "Behold this child is set for the fall and for the resurrection of many in Israel, and for a sign which shall be contradicted; And thy own soul a sword shall pierce, that out of many hearts thoughts may be revealed."*

— LUKE 2:34–35

The First Sorrow can be likened to the first sword that pierced Mary's heart as she came to recognize the sacrifice that her dear son would make for the world. Mary knew that God's grace is such that he will not inform us of all the crosses we are likely to bear in our lives, otherwise we'd feel defeated by the mere thought of the future trials we face. However, because of Mary's immaculate heart, she had intimate knowledge of how Jesus would suffer. She was able to hold this awareness alongside a profound trust in God's will. Throughout her unconditional love for her son, she was also aware that he would someday be persecuted and murdered by those who were threatened by his radical message of love and salvation. This is what makes Mary's suffering so poignant; the joy of being the Mother of Our Lord was always balanced against a constant recognition that not only was his life in danger, but it was also God's will for Jesus's death to be a testament to the depth and redemptive power of his sacrifice for the salvation of humankind.

At the time of the First Sorrow, Jesus was a newborn, and Mary and Joseph were new parents. The custom in Israel was for all parents to present their firstborn who were male, and after 40 days, to God in the temple to be blessed. Mary and Joseph did so out of respect for the custom, despite the fact that they recognized Jesus was no ordinary baby. He did not need to be blessed, as he was both the blessing and the one doing the blessing!

Mary was already aware of this, as her pregnancy was a miracle. As most people know, Mary received a visit from Archangel Gabriel, who had a message from God. Gabriel greeted Mary unusually: "Hail, Full of Grace, the Lord is with you." Mary was troubled and afraid, but the angel calmed her and said, "Do not be afraid, Mary, because you have found favor with God." The angel informed her that a most remarkable thing would happen to her—because of her virtue and love for God, she would give birth to the Son of God, who would be great among all nations and whose kingdom would have no end. At this time, Mary was already engaged to Joseph, but surprisingly, she didn't say to Gabriel: "I already have a fiancé. He isn't going to be very happy about this." Mary's allegiance, first and foremost, was to God, so she asked, "Because I have never known [been physically intimate with] a man, how will this be possible?"

Archangel Gabriel calmed her and told her, "The Holy Spirit will come upon you, and the power of the Most High will overshadow you; therefore, the child to be born will be holy; he will be called the Son of God." The angel told Mary that she would name him Jesus. (Yeshua is actually the Hebrew name for Jesus; when it is translated into Greek, it becomes Jesus). Her pregnancy occurred through the grace and power of the Holy Spirit (the creative spirit of God, through which everything is made). Yet, she remained a virgin. From the very beginning, Mary accepted the task at hand and knew that nothing is impossible when it comes to God's will.

She replied to Gabriel, "I am the handmaiden of God. Let his will be done in me."

It was said that when Mary officially accepted this mission, heaven had been waiting for her answer. God did not demand that she say yes, and it was important that Mary offer her wholehearted consent, as being the Mother of God was certainly not a role to take lightly! When she said yes, angels blew trumpets, and songs of joy were heard throughout heaven. It warms my heart to think of this deciding moment, a celebration that resounded throughout heaven and earth.

Because of Mary's faith and love of God, she had no hesitation in saying yes, despite the fact that appearing pregnant out of wedlock was punishable by death in Jewish culture. When Mary revealed God's plan to Joseph, he was immediately distraught. What would others say? How would they react? Because Joseph was a holy man, he knew he had to divorce Mary, but he planned to do it quietly so he would not expose her shame and cause her to be harmed in any way.

He attempted to break off their betrothal in secret. An angel of the Lord appeared to Joseph in a dream. He said, "Joseph, son of David, do not be afraid to take Mary home as your wife, because what is conceived in her is from the Holy Spirit. She will give birth to a son, and you are to give him the name Jesus, because he will save his people from their sins. Joseph, stupefied and humbled by this revelation, finally understood that it was his responsibility to care for Mary and their unborn child. So he, too, accepted his mission and took his young bride under his wing. This is how Jesus came into the world.

After Jesus's birth, when he was presented in the temple, Mary was excited, like any new mother. She was overjoyed at the birth of her child. Mothers were held in high esteem in ancient Israel, so she was expecting others to share their joy with her, to comment on how beautiful her baby was. Because she would be presenting Jesus to a high priest 40 days after his birth to fulfill the requirements of the law set down by Moses so long ago, she thought that perhaps the priest would recognize the Son of God and rejoice alongside her.

However, an old man named Simeon was present in the temple. According to scripture, Simeon had received a revelation that he wouldn't die until he'd seen the Messiah, the awaited redeemer of the Jews sent by God himself. Luke 2:28–35 recounts:

> Then he took him into his arms, and blessed God, and said, "Now Lord, you are releasing your bond-servant to depart in peace, according to your word. For my eyes have seen your salvation, which you have prepared in the presence of all peoples, a light of revelation to the gentiles and the glory of your people, Israel." And his father and mother were amazed at the things which were being said about him. And Simeon blessed them and said to Mary, his mother, "Behold, this child is appointed for the fall and rise of many in Israel, and for a sign to be opposed, and a sword will pierce even your own soul—to the end that thoughts from many hearts may be revealed."

Every time I read about Simeon's prophecy foreseeing the Crucifixion, my heart breaks. I think of Mary's motherly hopes for her beloved child, shattered by the somber words of Simeon. I imagine her fear and sadness. I imagine her limbs trembling, her breath becoming more labored, her mouth dry as she reaches out to Simeon to take baby Jesus back into her arms—to envelop him in maternal protection. I can imagine Mary feeling the world falling around her shoulders.

It is difficult for any mother to know that her child will live through struggle and suffering. It must have been even more difficult for Mary to hear this about her baby—and to understand that these were not mere speculations but facts that were coming through a prophetic revelation. This was not a case of a mother nursing minor worries about the fate of her child; in Mary's situation, she was already preparing herself for what was to come.

# THE DREAD OF DAYS TO COME

When I was pregnant, I couldn't even bear to watch TV shows about children who were born with illnesses or handicaps. I would love my child no matter what, but it troubled me to think of the possibility of his or her suffering. I myself had already lived through so much trauma, being one of the only survivors of the Rwandan genocide among all my other family members—I did not want to imagine anything horrific happening to my future children.

In thinking about Mary's First Sorrow, I am also reminded of the moment I learned that the president of Rwanda, Juvénal Habyarimana, had been killed. He was the second president of Rwanda (1973–94) and was nicknamed "Kinani," which translates to "invincible" in Kinyarwanda (one of the official languages of my country). Habyarimana was an ethnic Hutu who overthrew Rwanda's first president, Grégoire Kayibanda; however, like his predecessor, Habyarimana was in favor of policies that favored the Hutus. He was a formidable dictator, and during his rule, Rwanda's government became a totalitarian one. The long-organized genocide against the Tutsis by Hutu extremists started minutes after he was assassinated in 1994. It is important to mention this, because he was killed by his people to find an excuse to kill Tutsis; it was not his death that caused the genocide but the preparations done before.

I still remember the day that my older brother, Damascene, informed me of the president's death. It was dawn, and I was just waking up. I could see Damascene's terrified face in the gray half-light of my bedroom, and I imagined the worst. "What is it, Damascene? Are the killers here?" I whispered. I could scarcely hear my own frightened voice.

During my third year of university, Radio Télévision Libre des Mille Collines (RTLM), which was broadcast from 1993 to 1994, was the new, ultra-popular radio station among extremist Hutus. It was little more than a radical hate machine, spewing out anti-Tutsi venom. It was always some disembodied, malevolent voice calling for "Hutu Power"—the catchphrase for Hutus to rise up against their Tutsi friends and neighbors: "These Tutsi cockroaches are out to kill us. Do not trust them. . . . We Hutus must act first! They are planning to take over our government and persecute us. If anything happens to our president, then we must exterminate all the Tutsis right away! Every Hutu must join together to rid Rwanda of these Tutsi cockroaches! Hutu Power! Hutu Power!" Now, as I saw my brother's frightened face, I remembered all those evil, hate-filled calls to action.

My brother said nothing. I could hear him trying to catch his breath while he stood in the doorway. When he finally spoke, his voice sounded like it was coming to me from the bottom of a deep well: "Get up, Immaculée—for heaven's sake, get up. The president is dead!"

"What? What do you mean the president is dead?" I cried out. I couldn't believe what I was hearing. Despite all his flaws, Habyarimana had promised to bring peace and equality back to Rwanda. How could he be dead?

"He was killed last night. His plane was shot out of the sky," my brother hurriedly explained.

The refrain from the radio replayed itself over and over in my head: "If anything happens to our president, then all Tutsis must be exterminated!" I jumped out of bed and searched frantically for something to wear. I pulled on a pair of jeans under my long green nightdress and was so flustered that I actually dressed in front of my brother, something I had never done in my life. "The president has been killed; someone's killed the president," I kept mumbling to myself in dazed disbelief. I pushed the curtains away from my bedroom window and looked outside. I'm not sure if it was my imagination, but I saw a sickly yellow haze settling over the village. It seemed as if the world was awaiting disaster. Even if I was not 100 percent certain of what was coming, my gut told me that it would be something terrible. It was a strange feeling. But the most bizarre thought kept coming to the surface of my mind. I asked myself what I would do when everyone was dead. I was angry at myself for even thinking such a thing. How could I be so selfish? I, like all my family members, was a Tutsi; if they died, I would die with them. Of course, many decades later, I realize that God was revealing to me that I would survive.

When I meditate on Mary's First Sorrow, I don't think back only on my own fearfulness in those dark days preceding the genocide. I think first and foremost of my mother. I think of her worrying about her children's respective fates, and whether any of us would ever truly be safe. I also think of my father's pain and the helplessness he likely felt in recognizing that he didn't have the power to protect any of us. I can't begin to imagine the burden of sorrow that my parents, who had some inkling of what was to befall our entire country, were carrying.

However, it is Mary's First Sorrow that connects me to all these memories, that enables me to reflect on the times in my own life when I and my loved ones experienced similar suffering and to put all in the hands of God as she did in her sufferings. Our Lady was well aware that her child would suffer, although she did not know the details or timing. She simply knew that Jesus, in his suffering, would transform history and save humanity. He would open a portal to salvation for all humans, who suffer because of our ignorance. So there was a bittersweetness in Mary's experience, for she would be a firsthand witness to her son's persecution, as well as to God's promise to all humanity. And although Mary was helpless to protect her son from his fate, it is believed that she was a constant presence in his life, because she understood that there is no greater healing balm (aside from the love of God) than a mother's love. She knew that no one else could possibly understand her son enough to offer relief from his pain, so like any good mother, she never missed the chance to alleviate it—even though she knew that she could not remove it completely.

Scripture tells us that Mary was a virtuous and purehearted woman. In my early years, I developed a close relationship to the Blessed Virgin. For some, God can be an overwhelming and intangible force who is not necessarily easy to understand, as he lives on a spiritual plane that is so much vaster than our earthly existence. However, Mary was always an approachable presence to me. My parents were devout Roman Catholics and passed on their beliefs to us. Mass was mandatory on Sundays, as were evening prayers with the family at home. I loved praying, going to church, and everything else to do with God. I especially loved the Virgin Mary, believing that she was my second mom, watching out for me from heaven. I didn't know why, but praying made me feel warm and happy.

She was a comforting presence to me in the most difficult and terrifying time of my life, the genocide. During the frequent searches the killers made while hunting for me, every second I spent crouching in my secret bathroom hideaway seemed to last a year. But the moment I opened my heart to God in prayer and felt the protective hand of the Blessed Virgin Mary on my shoulder, I was transported to a place of peace where time ceased to exist, my heart was touched by eternity, my fear replaced with forgiveness, and my doubt dispelled by the certainty that I would forever be a beloved child of the Lord.

Mary was the human embodiment of love, kindness, and righteousness. She offers a glimpse into our human potential when we allow our love for God to lead the way and to dictate our actions in the world. Unfortunately, people like Mary and Jesus are not often greeted by humanity with open arms and heartfelt trust. Rather, they are hurt, humiliated, condemned, and sometimes even killed.

During the genocide, I often wondered why it seemed to be so difficult for people to see others as they really are. Why were people oppressed and murdered for no reason other than their ethnicity or the color of their skin? Why did humans behave so unjustly toward one another? Why did bad things happen to good people? With little else to do except pray and think about the sad state of affairs, I asked myself many questions just like these. I could recount the facts to myself, but I couldn't wrap my head around why any of it was happening. I came to the conclusion that injustice and sin had always existed because of human wickedness and the inability to see and act with clarity and love. I realized that while others may not see us or treat us with the goodness we all deserve, only God can penetrate to the core of who we truly are. Only God fully knows the contents of our hearts and only he is the just judge. I was made aware and I hungered for heaven—for paradise, where there would be no more pain or hate, and I wanted to work for that place.

## LESSON: BE WITH UNCERTAINTY

If you ever find yourself in a situation where you are not certain of the future (a position so many of us find ourselves in today, given the political, social, and environmental threats that seem to be closing in on us from all sides), think of what the Mother of God suffered, of the secret she carried inside her for 33 years, not knowing when it would come to pass but still knowing it was coming, and offer all to God as she did.

Imagine how her heart must have felt whenever she saw Jesus falling, or climbing a tree like any other boy. Perhaps she thought to herself, *It's happening now*. Imagine the silent reassurances she may have given herself in knowing that she would someday lose him, but that his loss would be for a reason—it would be God's will, so that he could be the salvation for all of humanity.

If fear comes up for you—whether you are thinking of your own fate or that of a loved one or the world in general—remember that you aren't alone and trust the one who is your Father and who is almighty. St. Paul tells in the Bible, Philippians 4:6–7, *"Do not be anxious about anything, but in everything by prayer and supplication with thanksgiving let your requests be made known to God. And the peace of God, which surpasses all understanding, will guard your hearts and your minds in Christ Jesus."* This was the hope of Mary in her sufferings, and this is where she wants us to be. So often, we attempt to find security by reaching for certainty. We want to be certain that our loved ones will be safe and healthy, or that we'll have a stable job, or that the roof over our head will be present for years to come. However, no matter our circumstances, change is a natural part of life. Only God knows what is to come; what is in our power is to do the best we can, just today, moment by moment. Few of us are blessed with the gift of prophecy (God is compassionate enough to ensure that we don't know everything that will transpire—because if we did, we might be so busy worrying about the future that we forget to live in the present!), so part of the human condition is learning to live with the awareness that much of our existence is entirely outside of our control.

This is why I believe it's crucial to resist the urge to fight this uncertainty and bring our worries to God. St. Padre Pio reminds us, "In times of uncertainty, pray, trust, and don't worry." We simply cannot know everything ahead of time. We must accept our human weaknesses and limitations, and relinquish the need to know the details of our lives before they unfold. Rather than wasting our energy worrying about tomorrow, we can learn to be fully present and to respond to what life is revealing to us at this very moment. We can trust the Almighty God and leave what is outside of our control in his hands. All we need to do is our part.

Remember, Mary is always here to intercede on our behalf. I know this, because I know that my prayers did not fall on deaf ears. I know that she heard the pain in my heart, and that she responded accordingly. I encourage you to take Mary as a prime example of how we can respond to uncertainty in our lives. We can never erase all the pain in this world. There will always be trials and tribulations to contend with. At the same time, we can choose never to become embittered by our pain. We can enlist the assistance of Jesus and Mary, who will always answer our call.

When Mary gave us the prayer of the Seven Sorrows Rosary, it was not her intention to make us feel doomed to suffer. She did not want her children to sit in persistent hopelessness or to be resigned to an unhappy fate. However, she did wish to open our eyes to the reality of human suffering. Everyone suffers, even those who might be smiling and showing the world a cheerful facade. At the same time that Mary accepted Simeon's revelation, she understood that worrying about tomorrow would make her lose the grace of the present moment and the beautiful gift she had been granted: being the Mother of God.

On top of Simeon's revelation, Mary was alive during a time of great social, political, and religious upheaval, so she was no stranger to uncertainty. The Jewish leaders in Jerusalem were merely puppets of the Roman Empire. The spiritual leaders of the time were hypocritical and corrupt. A small minority of high priests and merchants lived opulent, luxury-filled lives, while almost everyone else suffered in poverty. Jesus was born into an extremely volatile moment in human history, meaning that Mary constantly faced the threat of losing him.

However, Mary does not want us to live with the sword of uncertainty dangling over our heads. She knows that true security rests in entrusting our lives to God and surrendering to his will for us. For even if we face all manner of danger, our souls will always be safely kept by Our Lord. I can imagine Mary consoling us: "I lived a peaceful life, even if I had things I was worried about, even if I cried and felt pain as you do. I know what it feels like to be there, but my children, remember that today I am the Queen of Heaven and Earth. Tell me about your suffering. Leave it in my hands! I will help you."

It is true that when we share our suffering with God, we experience a great deal of relief—because a huge reason that we suffer to begin with is that we are fixating not on something that is actually happening but on our fears of what might happen tomorrow. We tend to worry about everything—from our jobs, to our relationships, to our home life, to the precarious human condition. Our worries loom large in our imaginations and eclipse the joy that is available to us in this precious moment.

Matthew 6:33–34 says, "But seek first the kingdom of God and his righteousness, and all these things will be added unto you. Therefore do not worry about tomorrow, for tomorrow will worry about itself. Today has enough trouble of its own."

Fear and anger are our worst enemies, as these are sentiments that paralyze us and keep us from making wise decisions. If we can focus on what we have today—our present hardships and our present blessings—and handle it with wisdom and care, we have the power to change the future. However, if we choose to worry about tomorrow, we are powerless to act today. Likewise, if we choose to poison the moment with our anger and resentment, we lose the energy that is necessary to do something about it.

I have heard clergy and spiritual teachers say that instead of worrying for our loved ones—something that is difficult to refrain from doing, especially for those of us who are mothers—we can choose to send them our blessings and prayers instead. We can even choose to send our blessings and prayers to the people who might be responsible for creating an uncertain situation for us.

It is also useless to wallow in our anger and indignation, or to protest our suffering because we don't think we deserve it. None of us are above Jesus or the Mother of God—two beings who were without sin yet still suffered. So when I think of the First Sorrow, it helps me to make peace with my past pain, to relinquish any control I may believe I have over my future (a control that is illusory to begin with), and to surrender to God. I can accept my pain in the present moment yet rest assured that I have a comforter, a friend in heaven who makes all things possible. So instead of worrying, I make peace with the future and I pray about it.

When you are in pain, when you go through injustice, try not to wallow in anger or fear. Rather, think of the one who came before you, who loves you unconditionally—the one through whom all things are made possible. If you can't find a friend in the one who sees and knows all things, who knows your heart better than anyone, you will spend your life being disappointed in others, in how they treat you and those around them. You will find yourself in a constant state of reactivity to the unfairness and injustice of the world. But these are artifacts of human sin, which is a transgression against divine law and our truest nature. Everywhere we look, we will find sin—to the extent that sometimes we might even wonder if sinlessness, purity, and goodness are possible. However, if we befriend Mary, Jesus, God, and the angels, we will rest in the peace of being known for who we truly are—for the totality of our being. And ultimately, this is the only certainty we can count on in an uncertain world.

### A Prayer While Meditating on Mary's First Sorrow

*Dear Father, Thank you for choosing one of us, and raising a human being, a woman, our Mother Mary, so close to divinity, to be so close to you, to be pregnant with your only son, to teach him how to be in this world, to protect him with such loving devotion. You showed us how much you love us. I thank you for giving us such—choosing the best, a role model and a mother, to look up to. As you warned Mary of what was coming to hurt her and you helped her through her suffering, I beg you to remain close to me in my own suffering. In the tomorrow that is never so sure, please look after my life and my loved ones. For every family that is suffering, every family that is worried about their children, please come to their aid. I show you everyone who is worried—Father, help them. And you, dear Mother Mary, thank you for saying yes on our behalf. Thank you for teaching me to love Jesus. Teach me to love him more. I am sorry for the tears you cried, but I am glad that you never gave up. I am glad that you faced your life with such courage. In giving up the need for certainty, you placed your life in his hands. May I learn to do the same. Amen.*

## Reflection Questions

Contemplate the First Sorrow. Take some time to journal on or sit with the following inquiries.

1. Have you ever experienced dread for something you knew was coming in the future but that you were powerless to prevent? How did this impact you? Where did you find comfort or solace?

2. In general, how do you respond to uncertainty and the unknown, particularly with respect to suffering? What emotions come up for you (e.g., fear, anger, frustration, or something else)?

3. Do you find it easy or difficult to stay in the present moment? What helps to bring you back when you are preoccupied?

4. The next time you are worried about something, instead of fixating on it, try sending yourself, others, and the situation itself love. Reflect on Mary's First Sorrow and offer the prayer in this chapter. Notice how it makes you feel.

CHAPTER 6

# THE SECOND SORROW

## The Flight into Egypt

*And after they (the wise men) were departed, behold an angel
of the Lord appeared in sleep to Joseph, saying: Arise and take the child and his
mother and fly into Egypt: and be there until I shall tell thee.
'For it will come to pass that Herod will seek the child to destroy him.'
Who arose and took the child and his mother by night, and retired
into Egypt: and he was there until the death of Herod.*

— MATTHEW 2:13–14

Upon the birth of Jesus, Herod (or Herod the Great, as he liked to be called) was the king of Judea (the ancient name for Israel during the rule of the Romans). Historians recount that he was a cruel, power-hungry ruler who destroyed anyone he feared was attempting to take away his power or share his throne. He even killed some members of his own family because he believed they were plotting against him.

When a group of wise men came to Jerusalem shortly after Jesus was born, they asked Herod's people where they could find the newly born King of the Jews. They added, "We have seen his star in the East and have come to worship him" (Matthew 2:2).

When word of the wise men's whereabouts reached Herod, he sent for them and asked them questions about this new King of the Jews; he urged them to find the child so he could worship him as well. But Herod was lying. His real goal was to destroy the child, fearing that Jesus, even as a baby, would eventually take over his throne.

When the wise men went to see the infant Jesus to pay him their respects and offer him the gifts of gold, frankincense, and myrrh in honor of his blessed birth, God warned them about Herod's plot in a dream that all three shared. When Herod realized that the three wise men had not returned to inform him of Jesus's whereabouts, he became even more furious and ordered the death of every child in Bethlehem below the age of two. Certainly, he believed, Jesus would die among them.

During that time of turmoil, an angel of the Lord came to Joseph in a dream and bade him to take the child and Mary into Egypt, as they were in grave danger; should they stay, Jesus would be killed by the vengeful Herod. Joseph woke up at once, and the three of them left Nazareth and headed toward Egypt. They were a poor family, and as Mary explained to the visionaries in Kibeho, they left quickly and took very little food to eat and clothing to wear. Mary would recount to Marie-Claire how worried she was for baby Jesus. He was hungry and cold, as they didn't have enough resources to sustain them through the journey. Many times along the way, he was crying and inconsolable. The road ahead was treacherous and difficult. Mary explained that when the angel of God told Joseph to leave at once, they were not sure exactly where to go. They were forced to seek out directions and maintain a low profile, as they understood that Herod's soldiers were likely pursuing them. Because the angel of God had not given them clear directions, Mary knew they had to trust God and pray for their safety. They didn't have the same privileges and comforts as many of us in modern times, but what they did have was the awareness that God always hears our prayers—and even in the absence of comfort and ease, our prayers have power when they are offered with the utmost sincerity. Mary knew that God loves everyone, but he particularly guides those who love him and who treat others with care and respect.

When I contemplate the Second Sorrow, I often imagine Mary carrying baby Jesus in her arms, swaddling him in what little cloth she had and attempting to keep him close to her body for what little warmth was available. I imagine Mary, a new mother, literally running for her family's life. No doubt, she probably wondered how Herod could be so cruel that he would call for the execution of innocent infants. I think of the sleepless nights that Mary spent as she, Joseph, and their baby made their way to Egypt, probably traveling in the darkness so that others would not find them. I think of Mary ruminating over the prophecy of Simeon and telling herself, "I didn't know it would happen so soon. My child is still a baby!" I think of the grief she must have felt when she learned that hundreds, possibly thousands, of other infant boys were being murdered in order to ensure that the Son of God would be destroyed.

Of course, it is tempting to see Mary's story through our own human stories, but we must always remind ourselves that Mary was unlike any other human being in that she did not stop to ask, "Why me? Why my child?" She didn't stop to question or make sense of the madness, which turned what should have been one of the most celebratory periods of her life—welcoming the Son of God into the world—into one of the most nightmarish. She and Joseph were not asked to understand or judge; they were asked to *run*.

Mary was no stranger to suffering. Her suffering, in fact, began quite early, when her own husband-to-be doubted her virtue upon hearing that she was pregnant. And then, as some of us will recall from scripture, when it was time for Mary to finally give birth, she and Joseph were turned away by almost everyone, forced to take shelter in a stable. Because every place on earth belongs to God, it is striking to imagine that people had the heart to turn away the Mother of God—that the Creator of everything was rejected in such a cruel and thoughtless way. (This is a good reminder to treat everyone we meet with kindness, because Jesus is in everyone.)

God's willingness to make Mary and Jesus so vulnerable had a function, however. He was revealing something about the human condition that all of us know in some way; as I mentioned in the chapter on the First Sorrow, it is impossible to find security in the world in which we live, which is filled with ill fortune and people who have closed their hearts and minds to the truth. God gives all of us freedom to behave as we wish, as much as the love in our hearts allows us to.

## THE HATRED IN OUR MIDST

Many times when I pray on this sorrow, I can't help but think back on what happened during the genocide in Rwanda in 1994, especially when it all began that year in April. My mother, father, my brothers Damascene and Vianney, and our friend Augustine spent the entire day huddled together in our yard listening to the radio. The broadcasts from outside of Rwanda reported that ordinary Hutu citizens were joining government soldiers and Interahamwe militiamen (the main perpetrators of the genocide) in killing innocent Tutsi civilians; meanwhile, the local stations were encouraging Hutus to pick up machetes and attack their Tutsi neighbors. I felt like a lost little girl waiting for my parents to give me instructions. I thought that since they'd survived the many political upheavals and Tutsi massacres since 1959, they must know what to do.

The national radio station continued to warn people to remain in their homes, and we obeyed. We were too afraid to open our gate to find out what was happening on the other side of the fence. We placed ourselves under self-imposed house arrest, worried that stepping beyond our property line could prove fatal. My family didn't own a telephone, and even if we had, most of the phone lines in the country were down. We were completely cut off, except for whatever the radio told us. We sat listening to the horrific reports for hours, until I thought I'd go out of my mind.

Late in the afternoon, I pulled out my books and began studying for my exams.

"How do you do it, Immaculée?" Damascene asked. "Where do you find the strength to study? Why do you believe that there will even be a school to go back to?"

My brother had helped me shake my own despair only hours earlier, but now he, too, was hopeless. It was my turn to be strong. "Stop worrying," I said. "We'll get through this. If things get bad, we'll slip across the border. Mom and Dad have been through this before. Have faith."

The truth was that I had little faith myself—I wasn't studying to prepare for exams, but to keep my mind off my family's worries.

That night, my father told me he was concerned for my health. "You haven't slept at all, Immaculée. The rest of us are going to stay outside tonight with the others, so I want you to go to your room and get some sleep."

"But Dad, I . . ." I didn't like the idea of staying in the house alone. I was terrified that we'd be attacked in the night.

He saw my hesitation and smiled. "Don't worry, my sweetheart. I'm here, and I'm going to protect you. It's cold outside, and you need to get some rest. Now go inside and lie down."

I knew that he couldn't protect me against the Interahamwe, but I couldn't bear to hurt his pride, so I did as he asked. My mother promised that she'd stand guard over the house to make sure I was safe.

Despite my parents' love and concern, I couldn't sleep at all that night either. I kept a small radio on my chest, spinning the dial until dawn and listening to report after report of what was happening around us. The news got worse as the night wore on: Tutsis were being killed in large numbers in every corner of Rwanda. In the middle of the night, I went outside and found my mother asleep in the courtyard. She'd dozed off guarding our front door. When I moved closer to wake her, my breath caught in my throat.

She was wrapped in a white bedsheet, and in the cold moonlight she looked like a corpse. I was overwhelmed by the sight and ran back to my room. I fell onto my bed, and for the first time since our nightmare began, I burst into tears.

"Why is this happening?" I cried into my pillow. "What have we done to deserve this? Why is being a Tutsi so wrong? Why are you letting this happen to us, God?"

I felt selfish for crying and dried my eyes. *Silly girl*, I thought, *cry later. This tragedy is just beginning, and there will be plenty of time for tears.*

I returned outside just as the sun was beginning to rise over Lake Kivu and stood beside my sleeping mother. I softly stroked her feet and carefully unknotted the tangles in her hair. Mother was always so beautiful and proud of her appearance—she'd be mortified to be seen in such a state.

I kissed her cheek and gently shook her awake. "Mom, get up," I said softly. "It's cold out here. Get into bed."

As soon as she opened her eyes, they filled with fear and confusion. "Where is Damascene? Where is Vianney? Immaculée . . . you should be in the house getting rest. What are you doing outside alone in the dark?" she asked, struggling to get up.

"What are you doing out here, Mom?"

"I didn't want to leave you alone in the house, but I didn't want to be too far away from your father or my boys. I have to make sure everyone is safe."

"Everyone is safe, Mom. The boys and Dad are camping out with the others. Maybe things will get better today," I said, my heart aching from the pain etched on her face. She'd worked and sacrificed for us her entire life and spent countless hours worrying about our safety. Now she knew she couldn't do anything to protect us, and it was killing her. She seemed to have aged years during the past few days.

So much about the ensuing days after the start of the genocide pains me: my father's desire to protect all of us, my mother's worry for her family, and the struggle to find a good reason for why any of this was happening. I think of the pain I felt when I had to leave without saying good-bye to my parents—because it was too painful to do so. We pretended we would see each other soon after. I remember my father handing me a rosary, and I knew in that moment it was over. I would never see them again. I also think of how on my journey into hiding, like Mary, I started to walk through the bushes, as I was not sure if I would come across militiamen and meet my end. As I think about it, I even remember some pain I didn't realize I still harbored, such as the disappointment and anguish I felt over being rejected by my neighbors, who seemed to want nothing to do with me. I was marked as a Tutsi, and therefore treated as a pariah, so that I didn't even feel safe passing through the same street I'd walked thousands of times before.

More than anything, I recall the single question that would haunt me throughout this time, that I couldn't seem to merely chase away with a reasonable explanation, because there was no reasonable explanation: "Why?" I tried my best to understand the minds and hearts of the killers. Some of them were intelligent people, with Ph.D.'s and responsibilities in their communities. Many referred to themselves as religious and God-fearing. What were they trying to accomplish? What internal pain were they trying to alleviate? As much as I tried, I couldn't. I couldn't see beyond their wickedness, their sadistic need to hurt others and strip them of their freedom. I trusted too deeply in the human capacity to love, and it was difficult to come to terms with this kind of destructive hatred. Had it always been here in my village, lying in wait to pounce on us when we least expected it?

## LESSON: GIVE UP THE NEED FOR JUSTIFICATIONS—AND DO WHAT NEEDS TO BE DONE

During the genocide, when I was in hiding and thinking about my suffering, I believed that I was undergoing the very worst thing that could happen. I was beside myself with anger and grief, because I believed that I was innocent. And maybe I was innocent; but in retrospect, the worst thing was not what was happening—it was my refusal to accept that this could happen to me. Many times in Kibeho, Mary had asked us to accept our suffering, and I didn't exactly understand what she'd meant. Was she suggesting that we suffer without asking for help, or let our enemy hurt us without defending ourselves? Over time, I started to get it, though. Acceptance entails knowing what is happening and finding a way through your situation without blaming, complaining, or making excuses. You have to tend to your wounds rather than focusing on what or who caused the wound.

But just as I experienced during the genocide, all of us are attempting to make sense of our lot in the world. It can be easy to accept and take for granted the simple joys that come our way, but when we perceive that an injustice has been committed against us, or that someone else's irrational deeds have impacted our lives in terrible ways, it isn't easy to accept.

Most likely, when you have gone through suffering, you have also attempted to find justifications. You have asked yourself, "Why is this happening?" You've racked your brain for things that resemble good reasons. Most of the time, this is a losing battle. We find few answers that satisfy us, and we become agitated and even more frustrated, which is another source of pain.

Many times, we pity ourselves when we think of our suffering, and we even start to believe that we are the only ones who have gone through such an ordeal. We begin to believe that we are all alone in the world, and perhaps God doesn't even care about us. However, one of the great solaces in meditating on Mary's Seven Sorrows is that it reminds us that others are no strangers to pain. There is relief when we recognize that we are not alone. We are not the only ones who have ever known pain.

Admittedly (and I've been here before), the wicked part of us believes that if people go through something difficult, it's because they deserve it or they've done something to contribute to their own suffering. We cling to the notion that we have absolute control over whatever happens to us—from relationship breakups to illness to job loss to addiction. But this is a harmful tendency because it attempts to find reasons where there *are* no sufficient reasons. There is evil in the world, and we will never fully understand it. Neither can we fully understand God's will. At the end of the day, all of us are subject to suffering in this human condition—even the purest of souls.

The human mind will always look for a justification, but our reasons will always pale in comparison to the truth, which we can never fully understand with our rational minds. The truth belongs in a spiritual dimension that values love and faith over reason. The truth acknowledges that bad things happen to good people. However, the way we react to these things is what has the power to set us apart.

Often, when I meditate on the Second Sorrow, I think about what Mary, baby Jesus, and Joseph endured as they were fleeing their home—for no reason they could conceivably make sense of. Having experienced the genocide, and knowing that there are so many people in the world who are forced into hiding and exile due to circumstances over which they have no control, I am aware that human greed and wickedness can turn this world into a living hell. Many pure souls have experienced the most heinous conditions in situations of war, calamity, and illness. In recognizing the bigger picture of suffering, instead of wasting our time on finding justifications, we learn to use the agency we have to pray for God's protection, and to quickly respond to our circumstances as they arise.

There is a powerful lesson at work here. I often think of people I know who might have certain handicaps—perhaps they are blind, or deaf, or cannot walk. It is not their circumstances but rather the extent to which they have accepted these circumstances that defines them and their attitude toward life. For example, you might see a person in a wheelchair smiling and happy and functioning well, because they have accepted their lives. It isn't that they have suddenly eradicated suffering, but they have learned to accept it. There are still others who have a great deal of privilege but can't muster the strength to get out of bed, because they haven't learned acceptance. I feel for them, because I understand that lack of acceptance is its own unique brand of suffering. When we fail to accept our lives, we are often too occupied with blame or despair to do anything constructive about it.

Like Mary and her family, we can accept that bad things happen, even to good people, and our main focus can be on taking actions that correspond to our desire to live peaceful, God-fearing lives. We can do whatever is within our power to remain on the path of truth, to seek and do the will of God—even if that entails suffering. We can learn to listen for God's guidance, and to do what needs to be done. When I speak to the importance of doing what needs to be done, what I mean is that we must feed the soul as much as we feed the body. Many of us will do only what feels good and pleasurable, and shy away from what is difficult or requires sacrifice. However, many of the things that might feel good are not actually good for us. What feels good today might not feel good tomorrow. What gratifies us in the moment can have bitter consequences and weigh heavily on our future. This is why we are called to pray for wisdom and discernment so we can make choices that bring us joy and lasting peace, not a moment of pleasure or comfort that turns into bitterness the next day.

When we accept our suffering and give it to Jesus and Mary, we can experience the joy that comes from recognizing that they went through something similar to what we are going through. We are in great company, as Almighty God and the Queen of Heaven and Earth have our backs. Mary's Second Sorrow reveals a great deal about what she and her family had to go through together, so when we meditate on it we can also cultivate compassion for ourselves and all others who have been forced to respond to sudden changes that make little sense to them.

When we become embittered in our suffering, it is akin to suggesting to God that we don't deserve it. However, "deserving" is a moot point. God himself was subject to all manner of terrible suffering when he came to us in his fleshly form. To believe that we are above suffering, even though God took it upon himself to bear an unimaginable burden of suffering, is like rejecting God outright.

All of us are part of a complex web of choices; some of these are our own, and others have already been made for us. The Second Sorrow reminds us that we are not above God or Mary, as each of us is compelled to navigate a life that is rife with perils. So

I encourage you to sit in contemplation of Mary's Second Sorrow and to take comfort in the fact that even if you can never find a suitable explanation for your pain, it isn't necessary to do so. The most important thing you can do when it's difficult to make sense of your own life is to remember that you will always have a friend in Mother Mary. So just as a child would reach out to their mother, reach out to the Blessed Virgin and trust that she will offer you a helping hand throughout your ordeal. She will clear the way so that you can do what needs to be done.

### A Prayer for Working with Mary's Second Sorrow

*Dear Father, I thank you so much for sending us your son to die for us. I thank you for showing us that you are with us always, warning us in times of danger. I am sorry about how the world treated your son. Please help me not to be like Herod and hurt or treat anyone unjustly, and if I have done so without realizing it, in any small way, please forgive me. Forgive our world; forgive us for so many insults to the Holy Mother, whom you chose and trusted. Forgive me for my blindness to your truth, and for my lack of wisdom and discernment many times. Forgive me for constantly attempting to find reasons for my suffering, and for the arrogance with which I have determined who "should" suffer and who "should not." Dear Father, I ask that you fill my heart with compassion for all who suffer. I pray for anyone who is being chased away, anyone who is at war, who is hiding, who is in prison unjustly, even those who are there for seemingly good reasons; they are now paying for their sins, so please give them the wisdom to acknowledge the wrong they have done and to repent for it so they can reconcile with you. I also pray for those who have hardened their hearts to the suffering of their brothers and sisters, those who cause pain to others without care. I pray for those who have forgotten their responsibility to you. Please have mercy on them and turn their hearts from evil. Amen.*

## Reflection Questions

Contemplate the Second Sorrow. Take some time to journal on or sit with the following inquiries.

1. Have you ever felt rejected or unfairly treated by those you trusted? Have you ever been troubled by the actions of others in such a way that you found yourself seeking the cause of their behavior? Do you still feel anger or hurt?

2. Do you find yourself constantly asking why things are the way they are? Are there times when your need to understand seemingly inexplicable situations creates more harm than good?

3. How easy is it for you to accept the way things are, even if they are difficult? What is the value of acceptance? How is it different from resignation?

4. Can you recall an occasion when you nourished your soul by doing what needed to be done, even though it was difficult?

5. The next time you find yourself angry at how things are and trying to come up with reasons for why things are the way they are, or why evil exists in our world, see if you can pull yourself out of the mental chatter and take positive action that moves you in the direction of God's will and God's love. Reflect on Mary's Second Sorrow and offer the prayer in this chapter. Notice how it makes you feel.

## CHAPTER 7

# THE THIRD SORROW

### The Loss of Jesus

*And having fulfilled the days, when they returned, the child Jesus remained in Jerusalem; and his parents knew it not. And thinking that he was in the company, they came a day's journey, and sought him among their kinsfolk and acquaintance. And not finding him, they returned into Jerusalem, seeking him.*

— LUKE 2:43–45

We know from the book of Luke that every year Jesus's parents traveled to Jerusalem to observe Passover. When Jesus was just 12 years old, his family made the long journey in accordance with the custom. When the festival was finished and his parents were returning home among friends and relatives, unbeknownst to them Jesus was not in their group. He had decided to stay in Jerusalem. In fact, Mary and Joseph traveled for a full day before they realized that their young and spirited son was not among their traveling party. Mary was beside herself with panic; together, she and Joseph immediately went back to Jerusalem to search for their beloved son. They looked for him for three days until they found him—cool, calm, and collected—in the temple, sitting among teachers and scholars, asking them questions and listening in rapt attention to their responses.

As scripture indicates, the teachers were astounded by this young boy's understanding of God and religious custom. He was clearly wise beyond his years, which is why they were gathered around him in the kind of conversation that could go on for days. Mary and Joseph were astonished when they saw him. Mary approached Jesus and said, "Son, why did you do this to us? Your father and I have been so anxious, and we've been looking for you for several days."

Jesus, clear-eyed, considered his mother and responded, "Why were you searching for me? Didn't you know I had to be in my Father's house?" At this time, Mary and Joseph did not fully understand what he was saying. Without attempting to argue the point, Jesus obediently went with his parents, and the three of them made their way home to Nazareth. As the Bible notes, "But his mother treasured all these things in her heart. And Jesus grew in wisdom and stature, and in favor with God and man."

Every time I think of this story, I experience a number of vivid emotions. I think of Jesus's wisdom and palpable thirst for connection with God, which fills my heart. I also think of his thirst for other people's salvation, such that he felt compelled to stay behind and speak to and question the scholars and teachers in the temple, all in order to enlighten them in the ways of his Father. Because this is Mary's Third Sorrow, I can also imagine the pain and consternation that she held as she searched frantically for her son for days on end. While I can't imagine the difficulty she must have encountered as she searched the homes of friends and the faces in crowded marketplaces for any sign of her beloved son, I too am a mother, so I have had minor inklings of the same experience.

When my son was three years old, I lost him in a grocery store for only two minutes. For those two minutes, I was a wreck. Despite the fact that he had slipped through my attention and moved only to the next aisle, those two minutes felt like an eternity. I could sense my heart dropping into my stomach. I was now someone I didn't recognize. My vision was blurry, and I couldn't see very well. I felt like I was moving underwater, and my grasp on my sanity was quickly loosening. I began calling for help from strangers. Even when I located my son, I'd worked myself into such a frenzy that my heart was still racing, despite my relief in finding him.

In describing this moment, I recognize that what I felt for two or three minutes, Mary felt for three entire days.

As I meditate on the Third Sorrow, I picture Mary: her shallow breath, the dark circles under her eyes from lack of sleep, the gauntness of her cheeks because she couldn't bring herself to eat, the constant stream of tears that fell down her face. I know that because Jesus was Mary's only child, she must have been especially worried for his safety. But more than this, Jesus was no ordinary child. Mary herself understood that he was God's child, and that she had been tasked to care for him with every fiber of her being. Mary was a beautiful, virtuous woman whose goodness extended to her mothering, but in that moment I am sure that Mary was berating herself for losing sight of her son for so long. In those three days, I am sure that Mary's heart vacillated between hope and despair. With every door that opened to her, perhaps she held on to the possibility that she would find her son; and with every door that closed after she was told that Jesus had not been seen or spotted, her heart probably ached at the prospect that she might never see him again.

I am certain that Mary sent her prayers directly to God, even as she agonized over Jesus's absence in those three days. I am also certain that the joy of being reunited with him likely assuaged the pain of his loss. Yet this experience was a preparation for what would come in the future. Mary knew from Simeon's prophecy that she would not always be able to guarantee her son's safety—and the Third Sorrow was yet another reminder of what lay in wait.

At the same time, Mary eventually came to understand that Jesus was exactly where he needed to be. He remained in the temple and risked hurting his mother only because he understood that the elders in the temple needed to hear from him. His presence and the gift of his wisdom were a balm for their souls. And while Mary suffered for three days, Jesus was aware that these people could very well have suffered for eternity. Mary was blessed to be the Mother of God, but the Third Sorrow was also a reminder that Jesus's mission on this earth was very large indeed. Jesus as God, even at a tender young age, felt a deep responsibility to those who needed him. And given that God loves all of us, he was where he was needed most.

And of course, in a very different way, when Mary steadfastly searched for her son for three whole days, she too was where she needed to be the most.

## THE PAIN OF SEPARATION

I am reminded of a time when I was a child and my mother and father took my oldest brother, Aimable, to the doctor because he was extremely ill. My parents stayed with my brother for three days. As they left, their attention was totally fixated on his well-being, and ensuring that he received the proper care. They didn't seem to be thinking that deeply about the three younger children they were leaving behind, all of whom were left alone at home without much protection. They simply had faith that everything would work out, that a neighbor would stop by or that we ourselves would seek and find whatever we needed. They didn't have time to think, for if they didn't leave at once, my brother would have died.

The rest of us children managed on our own. We understood that our parents had chosen to be where they were needed most. My older brother, Damascene, who was 12, quickly took charge and brought all our beds into the living room. We all slept together, ensuring that we were safe and secure in one another's company. My father's godchild, who was slightly older than the rest of us, also came to the house to make sure that we were all right. For the next three days, we camped out in the living room and managed the cooking and household chores together. In our togetherness, we felt protected. Just as our parents were exactly where they needed to be, so were we.

However, it is also true that while desperate times call for desperate measures, many people will be shortsighted in their interpretation of what is actually happening. It's possible that some people in my village might have blamed my parents for being irresponsible by leaving us children alone. In my language, Kinyarwanda, we say that when a cow falls down, every other cow will try with their horns to push it down even further. Anyone who falls will have somebody who turns a critical, judging eye upon them without even knowing the facts. Mary and Joseph were in a tenuous position. Perhaps you can picture their neighbors criticizing them for having neglected their son, for not having even noticed his absence. Perhaps some of them whispered behind their backs: "Jesus is not here. Where were Mary and Joseph when he was lost?"

Like any mother, I am sure she was beating herself up for not watching him more closely. At the same time, Jesus was at the age at which parents would trust a child to be somewhat independent—to walk to school alone, fetch something from a neighbor, or run errands by himself. The same was true for my siblings and me. We had grown up in a small village, and I'd never heard of children being poorly treated or kidnapped. I can imagine that in Jesus's time, people were simple, trusting, and protective, and that Mary and Joseph didn't feel the need to keep a tight leash on their child. At the same time, as a mother, Mary had a strong awareness of everything that could go wrong.

When I think of this sorrow, I can't help but think of what so many of us go through on a daily basis; some of us lose a loved one for two minutes in the grocery store, or for years to the influence of drugs or other circumstances that take them away from the path of God. Others might be kidnapped or trafficked, which causes terrible suffering to them and their loved ones. Sometimes we are in the presence of a loved one but they feel lost somehow, as if their soul has vacated their body. They refuse to share what is in their hearts, and we cannot reach them. Still others of us experience the anguish of mourning a lost loved one, as we wonder what happened to them and whether we will ever see them again. In all these situations, somebody is lost and cannot be reached.

My heart goes out to the loved ones of missing persons, because it is a tremendous source of suffering to bear this kind of loss. The reality of not knowing can feel like hell to live through. If you are in a situation like this, please put yourself in the hands of Our Heavenly Mother, who knows what it feels like to be there. Pray, pray, and pray some more. Trust that she has the power to intercede for you. Mary knows and sees what we ourselves cannot.

Personally, when praying the Third Sorrow, I tend to think of the pain my mother likely felt when my family members were abruptly separated during the genocide. We didn't even get to say a meaningful good-bye to each other. In the remaining days after our separation, my heart ached as I thought of my poor mother and what she must be enduring. When I was a child, no one else in our village had a motorcycle, and Mom always worried that Dad would be waylaid by bandits on a lonely mountain pass. Fretting about her family was one of my mother's main preoccupations, to the point that whenever any of us was away from home for more than a night, she'd listen to the obituaries announced on the radio every evening.

"Mom, think of all the good things that could happen to us instead of dwelling on what might go wrong," I urged her, albeit unsuccessfully.

"Oh, Immaculée," she said, "I couldn't bear it if someone knocked on the door with bad news about one of my children or your father. I just pray that I die before any of you do." She prayed incessantly for our health, safety, and well-being. She was the kind of loving woman who would still tuck you in bed even if you were 20 years old. Up until our separation, there was not a day that passed that my mother didn't have an idea of where I was and what I was doing. Even when my siblings and I lived in a boarding school, we knew to inform her if we left school or if we were with friends or family members. Tears never fail to come to my eyes when I think of my mother—bereft and helpless, her anxiety at a fever pitch—not knowing where her children were, if we were safe, or if she would ever see us again.

When I find myself lost in thoughts of the past, I remember Mary and Jesus. They seem so close, so near to me—dear friends and divine confidantes who can see what lives in my heart and who know exactly how to soothe the suffering.

Whenever I say this prayer, I feel so light and so loved.

## LESSON: KEEP YOUR HEART OPEN, DESPITE YOUR LOSSES

I know that like myself, there are probably times when you have felt close to giving up. You lost something or someone, and you didn't know whether you had the strength to continue. You wondered if it was worth it to keep trying; perhaps you felt resigned to your sorrow because you doubted that you could remain with the uncertainty or fully feel the pain and fear within your experience.

But think now of what the Blessed Virgin felt when she lost her child for three days—in a time when what was lost could not be located with the help of telephones, Internet, or organized law enforcement that might send out a search party for a missing child.

The Third Sorrow is an opportunity to familiarize ourselves with the very human element of loss—not just of the existential kind, but the kind that sends us into a flurry of activity, punctuated by hopelessness. The kind of loss that is endured by a mother who has suddenly been separated from her child. It can also help you to open up to any small loss you might have endured, such as separation from a dear friend, or sadness that comes from simple life transitions. When we meditate on this sorrow, we might be surprised to discover these hidden sorrows that we buried in our hearts, and to finally let them go.

Mary does not want us to deny pain and loss, no matter how small they might be, as an aspect of our humanity. She does not ask us to feign a strength that we do not have. Rather, the Third

Sorrow is, just like the other sorrows, an opportunity to consider how we can meet the trials of our lives in the same ways that Mary did.

Rather than lamenting your fate, blaming yourself or others for your loss, or dwelling on your mistakes, you can approach the situation with an open and trusting heart—which will mean opening up to your pain rather than distracting yourself with any of the aforementioned activities. Of course, as a mother, Mary felt pain at her son's loss, but I am sure that after they were reunited, she understood that she had to go through this experience. She knew that God could have protected her from this sorrow, but he chose to let her experience what every human being does. She must have come to the understanding that Jesus remaining in the temple was more important than reassuring his mother or salvaging her from maternal worry. After all, Jesus had come to this world to evangelize and help others to understand the truth. All earthly suffering comes to an end, and heavenly joy lasts for eternity. Jesus wanted everyone to know this intimately. God knew the purity of Mary's heart, so he understood that she could bear having her comfort sacrificed so that Jesus could fulfill his mission on this planet.

As human beings, many of us undergo great loss on a daily basis—loss of what we love and what lights up our life with meaning. This also reminds me of the story of Job from the Old Testament. Job is a devout man who is stripped of everything he holds dear: his health, his wealth, and his children. His wife angrily tells him to give up his faith, which he holds on to. She tells him to curse God and die. He does not. Although Job is never told why he is suffering, he comes to understand that God is omnipotent (all-powerful) and omniscient (all-seeing). God knows all, and his perspective is not one that we humans could possibly understand. Job's life is ultimately restored, and he is given even more than what he previously had.

Just like Job, Mary knew that God always has a purpose for his children who are suffering. When I think of Mary's response to her missing child, I am struck by what I imagine to be her gentleness in the midst of this struggle. It begs us all to ask the question: When we are frightened and we have lost someone we love, when someone has broken our heart—in our rush to fix what is happening, do we carelessly hurt other people? Or are we capable of remaining pure? Can we search for our loved one without seeking to blame or victimize others, or make them look evil?

Meditating on the Third Sorrow will help you to honestly search out the places in your own life where you have endured loss. What did that loss turn you into? Even in the midst of such pain, were you able to let your broken heart break you open to the possibility of goodness, courage, and patience?

If you are currently enduring the loss of a loved one or of something that is very dear to you, I advise you to take Mary's story as an example. Despite your losses, keep your heart open to God and pray for help. In Psalm 147:3, King David reminds us, "God heals the brokenhearted and binds up their wounds." And don't give up! Keep seeking, but do so with kindness. Don't focus on yourself alone; remember others and pray for them. Consider that for three days straight, Mary did not give up. She marched on with the endurance of a soldier (or, more appropriately, a loving mother). She did not feel sorry for herself or allow herself to be paralyzed by insecurities and worst-case scenarios. Those may have been present, but she never stopped looking for her son.

Even if you have endured loss or separation from those you love, never stop loving others. Perhaps the people whom you seek to be reunited with are out of reach, or they refuse your help. You can still find ways to love them and to be a beacon of unconditional support to the best of your ability. Above all, continue to offer your prayers for them to Our Lady and Our Lord. They understand what it means to suffer, what it means to be brought to your knees by the force of what you have endured. They also know what it means to heal.

Please always remember that God could have stopped his own suffering when he came down to this world as flesh—but he didn't. He understood that even his suffering had a beautiful purpose. So even if you have lived through what you consider to be extreme loss, know that this suffering has a purpose. Accept what has happened, but allow your hope and faith to be the fuel that enables you to keep going, to keep seeking. But do not seek with a desire for retaliation or punishment. Seek with love. Be courageous and allow yourself to be carried on the wings of grace when you are not strong enough to hold yourself.

While the temptation may be to pray for an end to our suffering, the truth is that all beings suffer on this earth. Instead of an end to our suffering, let's pray for a transformation of it. Mary endured betrayal, injustice, and the hatred of others. But throughout all this, nothing was truly "taken" from Mary. Her willingness to fully experience her suffering, rather than pushing it away or projecting it onto others, is what led to a transformation. Overall, Mary lived a short life on earth, and she certainly suffered, but her patience and love are what transformed her from a mere woman into the Queen of Heaven.

So, take heart. Even if your loved ones are not close at hand, the ones who love you most intimately and unconditionally are always watching over you, reminding you that you are never alone. And even if you never retrieve what you have lost, your ability to keep your heart open will bring you gifts that can never be taken from you.

## A Prayer for Working with Mary's Third Sorrow

*Dear Father, thank you for caring for us so much that you wanted to send your son and teach us the way to you. Jesus stayed in the temple, and you allowed it, because even if Mary suffered, she did so with the knowledge that it was for a reason—that it would be a blessing for others. Help me to bear witness to your truth and to face all danger with a steadfast awareness of what needs to be done—without fear of unfavorable circumstances or of another human being. Help me to steadily witness your word and be a fearless apostle of love and mercy. Help me to accept my suffering and not be afraid to bear whatever comes my way. Help me to never turn against you, against love, for any gain in the world. Give me wisdom and the necessary resources so I can represent you when you need me to. And dear Father, for all those who are confused and in search of a lost loved one, please come to their aid. Just as you helped Mary, please help them to bear their suffering and to have the wisdom to make discerning choices, even if these may seem contrary or ill-advised to others. Amen.*

## Reflection Questions

Contemplate the Third Sorrow. Take some time to journal on or sit with the following inquiries.

1.  Think of a time you experienced sudden separation from a loved one. How did you respond?

2.  Have you ever made an important decision that caused someone else suffering? Did this create conflict? Were you able to reconcile with that person, with yourself, with God?

3.  Thinking of the many people who experience prolonged separation from their loved ones (due to estrangement, conflict, death, drugs, war, etc.), how does it make you feel? Are there any gifts or lessons that can be gained from such an experience? Do you pray for them?

4.  If there is a loss you are currently dealing with (of a job, an identity, a relationship, a treasured object, etc.), sit and think about how you are currently dealing with it. Is there a sense of panic? Blame? Anger? The desire to take revenge? See if you can open your heart to God and seek his will in these situations and redirect your energy, including any ill will toward yourself and others, and ask yourself if it was Mary, how she could have dealt with the same situation. Reflect on Mary's Third Sorrow and offer the prayer in this chapter. Notice how it makes you feel.

## CHAPTER 8

# THE FOURTH SORROW

## Mary Meets Jesus on the Way to the Cross

*A large number of people followed him, including women who
mourned and wailed for him. Jesus turned and said to them,
"Daughters of Jerusalem, do not weep for me; weep for yourselves
and for your children. For the time will come when you will say:
Blessed are the childless women, the wombs that never bore and
the breasts that never nursed! Then they will say to the mountains,
Fall on us! and to the hills, Cover us! For if people do these
things when the tree is green, what will happen when it is dry?"*

— Luke 23: 27–31

Good Friday is the commemoration of the day Our Lord died
for us. All of the events leading up to this moment were precipi-
tated by the power that Jesus had accrued among the Israelites as
a prophet of God—as the Messiah himself. His teachings touched
the hearts of many people who yearned for a deeper understanding of God, and who had been alienated by the hypocritical
ways of the Pharisees, who claimed to be the upholders of tradition and quickly grew jealous of Jesus's stature as a teacher and
miracle-maker.

As it happens with many who profess the word of God and who come to bring deliverance to those who are cast in the shadows of sin, suffering, and ignorance, Jesus would pay the ultimate price: his life.

The priests and religious elders saw Jesus as a clear and present danger to their own authority, so they plotted to have him killed. They accused him of blasphemy, as Jesus had proclaimed that he was the Son of God—identical in essence to the Holy Father, but born into the world with a specific purpose. He was both God himself and the Son of God: fully human and fully divine. Jesus's power did not rest in orthodoxy or religion, but in something that was much deeper. For this reason, although he was a beacon of light to so many people who longed for a true connection to God, he was feared by those who believed his spiritual authority would supplant theirs.

To accomplish their plans, the men corrupted one of Jesus's apostles, Judas, who in his arrogance and weakness, disclosed the location of his beloved teacher in exchange for 30 pieces of silver. With this betrayal in motion, the men finalized their evil plans. Jesus had already foreseen that they would be coming for him, and he even prophesied the act of betrayal that would ultimately lead to his crucifixion. For an entire night before he was captured, he spent time agonizing in the Garden of Gethsemane; anticipating the pain and torture that were to come, he asked his Father in Heaven to change the situation. Again, the great mystery of Jesus's identity as both man and God is one that can never be fully understood; its paradox is meant to chase away our illusions of who God is, as our human limitations will always serve to conceal his true nature from us.

Ultimately, despite Jesus's fear, he quickly asked God for his will to be done in him. Jesus wanted to be an example of righteousness to others, despite the excruciating cost to himself; he wanted to show others what it meant to walk with and alongside God. To do God's will is to forget one's own; sometimes, this requires accepting suffering even if you don't want it, even if it hurts. Jesus became the sacrificial lamb for the sins of the world.

His willingness to be led to his death demonstrated that he knew what needed to be done. And through his recognition, he revealed that death is not the end.

Jesus was badly beaten before being taken by force to the Roman governor of Judea, Pontius Pilate. The men who had come for Jesus wanted him to be condemned to death. Word quickly spread that Jesus had been taken into custody, and so Mary quickly came to bear witness to the injustice. In many ways, amid the suffering she had already endured leading up to her son's death, I imagine that some part of her was prepared for this final ordeal. However, her awareness that her son would be martyred and that this was God's will surely did not mitigate her suffering as she watched this beautiful, innocent soul awaiting judgment like a criminal—bloodied, disrespected, humiliated.

Although Mary, as a woman and a commoner, had no power to appeal to Pilate's sense of reason and goodness, she remained hopeful that he and others would see through the lies and deceit and let Jesus go. Indeed, Pilate did sense that Jesus had been brought before him by fearful and opportunistic men, but his priorities lay elsewhere. Pilate found no fault with Jesus, but the crowds were demanding his crucifixion. Pilate was worried that if he refused to give in to their vengeful demands, word would reach Caesar. Although he attempted to release Jesus and even presented another prisoner by the name of Barabbas to trade places with him, the people would not be appeased. Pilate had no desire to get caught up in the affairs of the Israelites in a way that would have negative ramifications for his career and position, so he washed his hands of any responsibility and allowed Jesus to be taken to his death.

Pilate ordered that Jesus be tortured even further, almost to a point beyond bodily recognition. Jesus's tormentors then placed a crown of thorns on his head, pushing it in until blood coursed down his face. They mocked him, saying that this was a crown suitable for one who had been deemed the King of the Jews. Finally, they placed a heavy cross on Our Lord's shoulders, and Jesus was forced to carry this cross as he trudged through the streets of Jerusalem to Calvary (also known as Golgotha). This action is immortalized in the Stations of the Cross, a devotion that summons 14 moments during Jesus's journey to Calvary. It is a painful and important moment for us to recall. As Pope John Paul II once noted, "It was not lawful to condemn a Roman citizen to death by crucifixion: it was too humiliating. The moment that Jesus of Nazareth took up the cross in order to carry it to Calvary marked a turning point in the history of the cross. The symbol of a shameful death, reserved for the lowest classes, the cross *becomes a key*. From now on, with the help of this key, man will open the door of the deepest mystery of God."

As Our Lord carried the cross, he was mocked and spat upon by those who crowded around him with wicked glee. As he had little strength left, he fell down—not once, but three times. Still, those around him were merciless and pushed him to stand and bear the weight of the cross. Now, imagine his Mother, who was absolutely powerless in the face of the torture her son was facing. Mary had previously witnessed the love that Jesus inspired in all who encountered him, but now, even his previous followers had turned against him. Just as Jesus was betrayed by Judas, Mary felt betrayed—not only by Pilate, who had failed to honor the truth he knew and had refused to stand on the side of justice, but also by neighbors and friends alike, who had joined the mob in its loud insistence that Jesus be crucified.

Imagine, if you can, Mary and the few people who remained loyal to Jesus, such as Mary Magdalene and Jesus's apostle John— their entreaties to free Jesus drowned out by the spiteful screams proclaiming that he should die. Imagine Mary's horror at seeing the people around her transformed by the contagious disease of hatred. Perhaps they were so miserable that they wanted a scape-goat to blame for their suffering—something that would justify their own pain. I can see Mary in my mind's eye: she watches in horror as the people whom she believed to be her friends jeer at her beloved son, who struggles to hold up his own weight, much less the weight of the heavy wooden cross. Like any mother, she must have felt condemned alongside Jesus. But gracious and steadfast as ever, she kept that sorrow in her heart and watched. I know that Mary would have exchanged Herself with Jesus in an instant if she had the power to do so. Every mother wants to save her child from emotional and physical suffering; to see one's own child in such a debased and wounded state is a kind of helplessness that no parent ever wants to live through. I am sure there were moments when Mary wanted to rush to Jesus's side, but it was not within her grasp to do this for him.

As Jesus was a man, he was not immune to suffering—but as God, he had the power to put an end to that suffering; he could have stopped the torture instantaneously, but he didn't. Jesus continued to love even those who mocked and scorned him.

The film *The Passion of the Christ* depicts a piercing moment between Mary and Jesus as he carries the cross while a crowd of spiteful onlookers gathers around him. Jesus makes eye contact with his mother for a moment; in desperation, she asks when he is going to put this madness to an end, as she wholeheartedly believes in his ability to do so. His voice barely discernible, he responds, "Mother, I make all things new." Although this encounter is not described in the Bible, it is a poignant scene that helps me to picture the moment when Jesus fully allows his mother to see him and understand the full extent of his power, even in the midst of such heartrending vulnerability.

Just as with the Third Sorrow, Jesus did not protect his mother from her Fourth Sorrow; he did something much more profound. In allowing her to meet him and witness him in these dire conditions, he gave her the privilege of drawing closer and being a witness to every detail of his suffering. It is a rare moment of intimacy that offers us some insight into the sacred bond between mother and son. Jesus did not attempt to hide from her or to appease her pain; rather, in just a few words, he offered her the reassurance of God's will.

Calvary is the site where the Gospels tell us Jesus was crucified. As Jesus made the trek to the place where he would breathe his final breath, Mary was with him every step of the way—feeling his pain with him, carrying the cross with him (emotionally rather than physically), and offering her strength and courage to him, even as so many others had deserted him. While Mary was in pain, she was not afraid to see his suffering. She wanted to be strong for Jesus, to let him know that there was one person who truly knew him, who would die for him. She wanted him to know that he was not alone, even if she had little power to make a difference.

In this moment, Mary was not only the Mother of God physically; she was the Mother of God in the domain of her heart and spirit. She would never forsake him. I can see her recalling the words of the prophets—words such as those in Isaiah 54:7: "He was oppressed, and he was afflicted, yet he opened not his mouth; he was like a lamb that is led to slaughter." Alongside these dark omens, she faithfully kept the words of Archangel Gabriel, who had come to her so many years ago: "Do not be afraid." And because she was without fear, she did not flee. She remained present with Jesus until the bitter end—with a mother's courage, fidelity, goodness, and unwavering faith. In the words of Luke 1:45, "Blessed is she who believed."

## MOVING BEYOND BETRAYAL

I am especially moved by the Fourth Sorrow when I think about the betrayals that I experienced during the genocide, when Hutus and Tutsis who had lived in harmony for as long as I could remember were suddenly at war—and Tutsis, a minority group, were met with enmity by people who had only yesterday been their friends and neighbors. As I wrote about in my book *Left to Tell*, my father ordered me—his only daughter—to run to a local pastor's house for protection after the Rwandan president was assassinated, which instigated months of massacres of Tutsi tribe members. Not even my small rural community was spared from the house-by-house slaughtering of men, women, and children.

I was fortunate to be offered protection by the pastor, along with seven other women. For three months, we huddled together in a small three-by-four–foot bathroom as the genocide raged outside. I will always remember being liberated from my hiding place; I was weak and barely able to stand, at only 65 pounds. But worse than my physical transformation was the news that quickly came my way: my entire family, with the exception of my brother Aimable, who had been studying abroad, had been murdered—along with more than a million fellow Rwandans.

The good pastor who had given me shelter handed us over to some French soldiers, who took us to their base camp 10 miles away. I was getting used to the newfound sense of space. Although we slept on the bare ground with not much to eat, I felt protected—something that I hadn't felt in a long time. The cool air brought goose bumps to my skin, reminding me that I was no longer in the cramped, humid bathroom. I stood up, stretched toward the sky, and then walked about the camp. I was completely unafraid, even when I stumbled across two men sitting in the shadows.

I startled them, and one jumped to his feet. After a second, he cried, "Immaculée, is it you?"

I quickly recognized him as Jean Paul, a young man who had been a good friend to my brother Damascene.

"How is it you're alive?" he asked, dumbfounded but clearly happy to see me.

"God has spared me. How is it *you* are alive?"

"God has spared me."

"It's good to see you!"

"It's good to see you!"

I wanted to laugh and cry at the ridiculous course of our conversation, and at how wonderful it was to be talking out loud to a friend again.

Although Jean Paul himself was extremely sorrowful, we sat down and exchanged stories. I told him where I'd been and described my time at the pastor's. Jean Paul told me that the genocide had died down a bit in the north since Kigali, the capital of Rwanda, had fallen, but it was still very bad in Kibuye province, where we were.

"Kigali has fallen?" I asked, shocked and delighted.

"Yes, but there's still plenty of killing," he replied. "In fact, around here it's even worse than before. The worse the war goes for them, the more vicious they become. They're getting frustrated too—they've slaughtered so many Tutsis already that they're having a hard time finding more of us to murder."

"The genocide is happening in people's hearts, Jean Paul," I said. "The killers are good people, but right now evil has a hold on their hearts."

I told Jean Paul that I would pray for his family. Then I realized that he probably knew what had happened to my parents and brothers, since he'd been in the area throughout the genocide. The question was: Did I want to know what had happened to them? Was I strong enough to take it? If I knew for certain that they were dead, there would be no going back to my old self, my old life.

I decided that it was better to face the truth. I'd have to pretend that I already knew my family was dead, otherwise Jean Paul would try to spare my feelings and tell me nothing. I'd have to trick him into telling me what I needed to know. I reached into my pocket for my father's red-and-white rosary and asked God to give me strength.

"So, Jean Paul, about my father . . . I know they killed him; I just don't know where. I was wondering if you might know any details."

"Oh yeah, I know everything. They killed your father in Kibuye town."

His words pierced my heart like a spear. I pushed my fists into my eyes and turned my face to hide my tears.

"Your dad was killed a day or two after my parents were murdered," Jean Paul went on. "He'd gone to the government office to ask the prefect to send food to the stadium because there were thousands of refugees there who hadn't eaten for days. That was a big mistake."

*Oh, Daddy! Why did you have to be so sweet . . . and how could you have been so naive?* The prefect of Kibuye was like the governor, and he'd been close to my father. But other extremist Hutus who were Dad's friends had betrayed him, so I couldn't understand why he continued to trust them. But I knew that he would have sacrificed his life trying to feed starving people—for him, there would have been no other choice.

"And what about my mom? I know she was killed too, but I don't know how—"

"Oh, Rose?" he broke in. "She was one of the first in the area to die. She was murdered a few days before your father. She was hiding in the yard of your grandmother's neighbor. Someone was being killed nearby, and your mom heard the screaming and thought that it was your brother. She went running into the road, shouting, 'Don't kill my child! Don't kill my Damascene!'

"It wasn't Damascene, but as soon as the killers saw your mom, they went after her. They told her that if she gave them money, they'd leave her alone. She agreed and went to borrow some from her friend Murenge. But Murenge ordered her to leave her alone: 'Get away from my house—we don't help cockroaches here!' Murenge told the killers to take your mother into the street to kill her because she didn't want them messing up her yard. They dragged your poor mom to the side of the road and chopped her to death. Some neighbors buried her, though. She was one of the few who got buried . . . soon there were too many bodies and no one left to dig graves."

It is still bewildering to think back to the moment of hearing this news from Jean Paul. Every word he uttered was torture. Part of me wanted to numb myself to what he was saying, especially as I thought of the people who had so quickly turned against my parents, despite the fact that they had always placed others' safety and welfare above their own. But when I meditate on Mary's courage in following her son to his bitter end, in making sure that she could take in every single detail of his final days, I recognize that we must always use our last ounce of strength to bear witness to great suffering and to stomach the betrayals of those who may have had the power to put that suffering to an end.

## LESSON: STAY FAITHFUL IN THE
## FACE OF BETRAYAL

Mary's Fourth Sorrow has always haunted me, because I know many people who were betrayed by those who had previously offered friendship and allegiance. During the genocide, the waters of brotherhood were poisoned by greed, fear, and convenience. When I think of the violence and sinfulness that can cause a person to turn against not just their fellow human, but against God himself, I come closer to understanding the many dimensions of Mary's experience.

Not only was her son suffering, but he had been severely betrayed—by Judas and his absent apostles, and by people who had only days previously, on Palm Sunday, greeted Jesus by spreading their cloaks out and laying palm leaves in his path to proclaim him the true King of the Jews. Coming to terms with such falseness and duplicity must have been very difficult for Mary. How could those who had expressed such love and devotion now be hurling insults and hatred at Jesus?

In Kibeho, the visionary Marie-Claire received a number of visions of Mary weeping inconsolably as she followed her son to his death. "Somebody help her—somebody help our Mother!" Marie-Claire cried out in agony as she received these visions.

In thinking of the fact that Jesus and Mary were able to bear their afflictions with so much dignity despite their loved ones turning against them, I am reminded that it is possible to bear our own personal crosses with honor rather than bitterness or the desire for revenge. As I consider the betrayal that I and countless other Rwandans experienced when our country was split in two by a militant appetite for destruction, I remember all the times I felt like giving up. But when I think of Jesus, who willingly gave his life for the world's salvation, and of Mary, who refused to close her eyes or turn away from her beloved son, I know that we cannot allow the betrayals of others to make us relinquish our faith.

Mary understood that Jesus, who could put an end to the misery, needed to allow fate to play out. In the meantime, her steadfast presence would be a powerful sign of her loyalty and devotion, in the face of such degradation. By this time in her life, Mary had already lost everyone she loved: parents, relatives, her dear husband Joseph . . . and now, she was about to lose Jesus. There is no greater pain I can imagine than a mother witnessing the torture of her child by people who have turned away from truth, love, benevolence, and godliness. However, it is the faith we maintain—through our pain, through our hardships, through our awareness of injustice—that has the power to keep our hearts pure. We can allow our suffering to be a purifying fire that burns away all ill will toward ourselves and others, rather than a sore that festers and spreads its poison to the people around us.

As I have mentioned in previous chapters, it is tempting to come up with justifications for the terrible things that have happened to us. It is tempting to want to play God and mete out judgments and punish wrongdoers. But we must not let our suffering get the best of us. We must not allow our suffering to debase us and bring us down to the level of those who have allowed sin to enter their hearts and poison the wells of their souls. And most of all, even if we have been betrayed, we must not betray ourselves or God. We must remember what is worth fighting for, what is worth giving our lives in exchange for, even if we believe that we have little power to change a difficult outcome. We must remember that others might harm us in the here and now, but when our hearts are pure and faithful, nothing has the power to touch us. We can enter eternity with the reassurance that even if we were wronged, we remained steadfast and continued on God's path although the light was dim and the road was long.

Believe me, I have encountered many moments when I thought my suffering was unbearable and I didn't think I could withstand it for much longer. But I continued, because I knew I could not give up on the ones I loved—including my mother and father, who had sacrificed so much in order for me to have a chance at life, in a time when it seemed that the worst had come and that few of us would survive it.

It is difficult to come to terms with our suffering when it is the direct result of someone else's ignorance, hatred, or betrayal. But even those who have been through war or genocide understand that such sickening and destructive conduct cannot crush our spirits if we hold on to God, who is powerful and all-knowing. Just as Jesus experienced the abrupt shift between the adulation he received on Palm Sunday and the torment that was heaped upon him on Good Friday, many of us have lived through severe betrayal. The wounds that betrayal can leave behind are strong enough to impact some of us for a long time, so that we continue to relive the most caustic and hurtful moments . . . sometimes, many years after the fact.

But our suffering is never futile. Even in the face of betrayal, it can serve as a reminder that the ones who truly love us will never give up on or turn away from us. Likewise, many people who have come face-to-face with the atrocities of war and genocide have allowed the purifying fire of their pain to reconnect them with what is good and eternal. Their experiences have taught them to rise above the worldly fears and desires that drive human folly and sin. Their experiences have enabled them to extend a helping hand to those they love, as well as those who may have wished them harm.

Betrayal, like suffering, is a reminder that all humans are fallible; many will choose convenience over righteousness. Therefore, surround yourself with good people who value truthfulness, authenticity, kindness, and godliness. At the same time, remember that Our Lord had Judas among his apostles. He knew Judas's intentions, but he chose to have him in his inner circle to show that we, too, will live and work among those who might betray us; therefore, we must be strong and wise, pray for them, and offer them to God. The Bible tells us to pray and love those who hate and persecute us. We will always meet those kinds of people on our path, and we will sometimes fall into their trap. Some of the people we will meet will be our crosses to bear. If that happens, don't beat yourself up for trusting them; rather, rise up, learn from it, and offer that suffering to God.

In contrast, a true friend is a gift from God, and they will never desert you in your time of greatest need. They will courageously walk beside you every step of the way. They will offer advice when you need it, but most of all, they will not forsake you. You will know a true friend not merely through the words they speak, but through their actions—through the consolation they offer in a smile, a hug, or a silent gesture of accompaniment. However, even a true friend is also human, so sometimes they will fall, disappoint you, or hurt your feelings. And sometimes we, too, will struggle to show up for others in their time of need.

It took unwavering courage for Mary to be present for and with her son, whom so many others had rejected in his darkest hour. All of us have experienced our own limitations in the face of wickedness, and all of us have felt helpless. But Mary is an immaculate example of what it means to cultivate and maintain our faith. She never broke her vow to God, to be his devoted Mother as long as he lived. Mary understood that it was impossible for her to protect Jesus, because he did not need her protection. However, I know he deeply valued her presence, her willingness to demonstrate her maternal love until the very end. Mary remained a dutiful, faithful, trustworthy friend and Mother to God—which is something each of us can try to do, to the best of our ability.

We can demonstrate our faith through our love for God and our willingness to live as he lived. As Matthew 5:38–39 states, Jesus proclaimed: "You have heard that it was said, 'Eye for eye, and tooth for tooth.' But I tell you, do not resist an evil person. If anyone slaps you on the right cheek, turn to them the other cheek also."

There is nothing passive about turning the other cheek. It is a holy, radical act to give up our defenses and to meet our enemies with an unwavering gaze and an open heart. It is an act of rebellion that reminds us of who we truly are—and that saves us from sinking to the level of our tormentors. It is an act that reminds us that God will never give up on us, so we must never give up on him. We must allow ourselves to be the pure vessels of his will.

Remember that suffering does not have to be a curse. It does not have to send us into fits of self-pity or dreams of revenge. God always offers moments of respite and relief. God will not let us suffer forever. Some heal their pain by inflicting it on others, which causes new pain; others heal in healthy ways, such as prayer or acts of kindness. If we are lucky, we will have dear and loyal loved ones who help us to take up our cross and remind us that we are not alone. And even if we feel that we have nobody, we can always remember that Our Mother is by our side, gently whispering words of maternal succor, gently reminding us that we will always have a friend in her.

### A Prayer for Working with Mary's Fourth Sorrow

*Dear Father, the world hurt your son when he came to save us, to love us, to give us life. Help us to remember and imitate the love and affection of Mother Mary when she met Jesus on the way to the cross, and when she stayed with him until the moment of his death. Help us to remember how they suffered together for my salvation, and let me love them both and be grateful for what they endured. Help me to remember their pain, patience, power, gentleness—and open my eyes that I might seek you all the days of my life. We so much want to be loved; we crave that others remain loyal to us. Help me to maintain my faith in only you, the author of all good things and of life itself. Even if others harm me or hurt my feelings, help me so that I never run from you. Dear Mary, you stood beneath the cross of your son, in such pain, while knowing that he was there willingly, out of love for us. I am sorry for the blindness of those who are led to betray, torment, and harm others. I pray for your mercy for a world that has lost its way. Amen.*

## Reflection Questions

Contemplate the Fourth Sorrow. Take some time to journal on or sit with the following inquiries.

1. Have you ever been scapegoated? Have you ever scapegoated someone else (including a group of people you might not agree with)? In thinking about these experiences, how do you feel? Can you resolve to ask God to forgive them, and to forgive you?

2. Think of a time when you felt deeply betrayed. How did you respond? As you consider that experience, what comes up for you? Can you bring yourself to pray for your enemy and ask God to change their heart?

3. Have you ever betrayed yourself by doing something that went against your moral code or integrity? What did you learn about yourself? God asks us to love others as we love ourselves, as you forgive others, also forgive yourself. God forgives always.

4. The next time you encounter someone who is in the midst of deep suffering that you do not have the power to alleviate (and this might be yourself), think of what it means to be a steadfast and loyal friend, to give them a hand, to offer a prayer or just be present. Reflect on Mary's Fourth Sorrow and offer the prayer in this chapter. Notice how it makes you feel.

## CHAPTER 9

# THE FIFTH SORROW

### Mary Beneath the Cross of Jesus

*They crucified him. Now there stood by the cross of Jesus, his mother.*
*When Jesus therefore had seen his mother and the disciple standing*
*whom he loved, he saith to his mother: "Woman: behold thy son."*
*After that he saith to the disciple: "Behold thy mother."*

— JOHN 19, L8:25–27

Mary's nightmare continued as she followed her beloved son to Calvary, where he was nailed to the cross. I have heard that before Jesus was placed onto the cross, he was stripped naked; a soldier with the decency to preserve Our Lord's modesty took Mary's veil from her and wrapped it around his genitals; this is the cloth that we see as we behold Jesus on the cross in most effigies. Ever faithful, Mary stayed with her son, refusing to leave him. As I meditate on the Fifth Sorrow, I can see Mary standing beneath Jesus on the cross, weeping at his anguish as she watches the life rapidly drain from his body. I can see Jesus shaking as the weight of his body is pulled down by gravity and the nails tear into his flesh. It is heartbreaking and almost unbearable to stand by and watch, but Mary is stubborn, as only a mother can be. She will never leave him alone in his time of profound agony.

Try to picture, if you can, what happened during this dark moment in human history as if it is unfolding before you. All day, Jesus has neither eaten nor drunk; after being beaten by soldiers, his body is covered with fresh wounds. Blood pours from these wounds, and he cries out in a state of constant agony. Mary, Jesus's disciple John (the only eyewitness at the cross among all the authors of the Gospels), Mary Magdalene, and Mary (the sister of the Virgin Mary) are standing faithfully before him. It is possible that Jesus's blood, which trails in dark rivulets to the ground, is falling onto them too. The stench of the crucifixion ground, where so many other people have been consigned to die a wretched death, is overwhelming.

I imagine that Mary's sorrow went beyond that of a passive bystander. Mary told Marie-Claire that she literally felt Jesus's pain in her heart and body, as if she herself were on the cross. The agony of watching the soldiers continue to torment and mock him, and for the dying man's request for water to be met with scorn and offerings of vinegar, must have sent an arrow straight through Mary's heart.

Throughout Jesus's ministry, it is likely that he spent a great deal of time traversing the region, giving his teachings, and healing the many people who flocked to see him. He probably didn't spend much time with his mother during this period, since he was busily fulfilling his purpose. It is heartbreaking to imagine Jesus and Mary being reunited, at the end of his public ministry, at the foot of the cross. Clearly, given the passage at the beginning of this chapter, Jesus was greatly concerned about his mother's well-being and the matter of who would look after her. Joseph died before Jesus's public ministry, and he is not present in the accounts of Jesus's life as a teacher and healer. It is an agonizing yet beautiful moment as Jesus entreats John to look upon Mary as he would his own mother, and to ensure that she is taken care of. In this moment, Jesus also entrusts Mary with the role of being mother to all humankind.

Both the Gospels of Matthew and Mark share that Jesus calls out one final time in the ninth hour, after three hours of darkness. "And Jesus uttered a loud cry, and breathed his last" (Mark 15:37). It is a cry that reverberates through the earth and skies, and in this moment, it is the cry of a man who feels utterly deserted by his earthly companions, as well as his Father in heaven. There is something deeply poignant in this story of God in fleshly form, feeling the same misery, grief, and separation that so many humans have approached in their final hour. Although Jesus does not remain disconsolate forever, it seems fated that he undergoes this initiation into the most horrific example of a human death. Mark even notes, unlike the Gospel of John, that Jesus's loved ones gazed upon him from afar—making the distance between Our Lord and the world around him seem even vaster and more foreboding.

Jesus is now completely alone and tasked to face death by himself.

My entire body trembles when I think of what Jesus was willing to be subjected to in order to transmute the symbol of the cross from one of terror and humiliation and into one that evokes the spiritual mystery of God's incarnation into earthly form. Every time I think of the Fifth Sorrow, I am also reminded once more of Mary's First Sorrow, during which Simeon offered the prophecy of Jesus's death when Our Lord was presented as an infant at the temple. Certainly, Mary feels the pit in her stomach as she considers that this prophecy, which has haunted her for so many years, is finally coming to pass. The wickedness of the world has overcome the secret hope she must have harbored that her son would find a way to bypass this grisly fate. She understands that for the past 33 years, she has been vigilantly anticipating the worst. Whereas the previous sorrows were signs of what was to be, they came nowhere close to the misery of this particular moment.

Mary watches helplessly as her son, the light of her life, fades away. Perhaps she vacillates between horror and numbness—because how can anyone possibly take in the enormity and significance of such a moment? Perhaps it feels as if evil has finally triumphed, and the sins of humanity have drowned out the humanity of the Savior.

However, as so many people have experienced in dire times, it is always darkest before the dawn. I Timothy 2:5–6 notes, "For there is one God. There is also one mediator between God and the human race, Christ Jesus, himself human, who gave himself as ransom for all." I Peter 2:24 also says, "He himself bore our sins in his body upon the cross, so that, free from sin, we might live for righteousness. By his wounds you have been healed."

We know from scripture that as horrific as the moment was, as much as Jesus's loved ones wished for it to be otherwise, as much as Jesus may have felt abandoned by his Father—none of this occurred in vain. It was part of a divine plan meant to open our hearts to the truth, and to forge a path of salvation for anyone who could recognize the extraordinary sacrifice that Jesus made.

The innocent lamb was brought to the slaughter so that all of us could be redeemed. It is a paradox that the Gospels capture with startling clarity, all the way from the betrayal in the Garden of Gethsemane, to Jesus's abandonment by his apostles, to Jesus being brought before Pontius Pilate and then to a trial before the Sanhedrin (the supreme council and tribunal of Jews, who had religious, civil, and criminal jurisdiction across Judea), to the unrelenting mockery and torture, to his subsequent suffering and death. However, even though darkness seemed to spread across the land, a heavenly beacon of light was being poured over the world. Jesus died willingly so we may have a life as prophet Isaiah 53:5 says, "But he was pierced for our rebellion, crushed for our sins. He was beaten so we could be whole. He was whipped so we could be healed."

As Luke 23:46 tells us, Jesus's final words are, "Father, into your hands I commend my spirit." Until the very end, the earthly Jesus offers his complete trust to his Heavenly Father. He moves into the experience of death with the same spirit in which he lived.

I often wonder how Mary was able to hold herself together while witnessing the painful, inevitable demise of her son. At long last, she understands that there is no possible way she can protect Jesus or turn the wheel of fate in a brand-new direction. But at the very least, she can bear witness to his suffering and assure him that she will never abandon him.

# THE MAKING OF A SPIRITUAL WARRIOR

What does it mean to be with the reality of human suffering in such a way that prompts us to stare directly into the face of evil rather than allowing our fear to get the best of us? I believe it is the force of love that helps to ground us in times that would knock anyone off their center.

As I think of Mary's experience, I can recall that fateful April day in Rwanda in 1994 when the government-backed Hutus came for the Tutsis. At dawn, the screaming began. Two dozen Interahamwe militiamen attacked our village, tossing grenades into houses. When the families inside attempted to escape, they were hacked to death with machetes. When my family heard the screams, we opened our gate and ran out onto the road. We could see for quite a distance from our hilltop home as we searched for the source of the commotion.

Below us, on the far side of a nearby river, we saw a group of Interahamwe surrounding one of our neighbors. They moved like a pack of jackals, holding their machetes above their heads and circling him slowly. We watched helplessly from afar as they moved in for the kill, mercilessly chopping him to bits.

We turned away from the murder in horror. Coming toward us quickly from the other side of the hill were dozens of our Tutsi neighbors. The men were carrying sticks and stones to protect their families, while the women carried their babies in their arms and yelled at their older kids not to fall behind.

"Leonard! Leonard!" they called when they saw my father. "Please help us. They're killing us! What will we do? Where should we go?"

Since my father was one of the most respected men in the village, within a few hours approximately 2,000 men, women, and children were camped out in front of our house, looking to him for guidance. I couldn't believe how many people had been driven from their homes. Scores of families sat around cooking fires, arguing about what to do next, while their children played games and chased each other through the fields. If it hadn't been for the occasional gunfire and grenades exploding in the distance, the gathering could easily have been mistaken for a family picnic.

The number of people who had come seeking my father's help and advice seemed to bring him back to reality. He became more like himself and took action. "Everyone be calm," he said. "We'll find a way to get through this together."

Very quickly after that, at least 10,000 Tutsis were camped in front of our home. My father was walking through the huge crowd, greeting people with words of encouragement. He'd been up all night and refused to go inside and rest. He washed, put on fresh clothes, and was right back among the refugees. Dozens of people were trying to reach him, calling out his name, but there were so many that it was impossible for him to talk to them all.

Finally, he climbed to the top of a large boulder at the base of a cliff and turned to the frightened crowd. "Friends, friends!" he shouted. His voice boomed above the multitude. "I know you're afraid; don't be. These people—these killers—are few, and we are many. They're not stronger than we are, not if we have God's love in our hearts. If they are acting out of evil, if they have come to harm us for no reason other than their hatred for us, then we will defeat them. Love will always conquer hatred. Believe in yourselves, believe in each other, and believe in God!"

My heart swelled with pride. It was hard to believe that this was the same man who had seemed so confused and unreasonable just hours before—in a state of bewildered denial as he refused to believe that we were in the midst of an actual genocide. Yet here he was, passing his strength on to so many lost and terrified souls.

As he told the villagers who had gathered around us, "If these killers are driven only by hatred, we will force them away. But if the government is sending them, if these attacks are part of an organized plan to exterminate Tutsis, we are in serious trouble—they will kill us. The government has guns and grenades, it has an army and a militia, and we have no weapons at all. To make matters worse, they've closed the borders of the country."

As he said all this, I felt afraid for him. He was telling a crowd of thousands that they very well might die. I was worried that they'd rise up and attack him.

He continued, "If the government plans to kill us, all we can do is pray. However, let's take this as a chance God is giving us to repent for our sins so we can go to heaven. Either way, do not be scared, for fear is the worst enemy of all. Let us pray for God to forgive our sins. If we are to die, let us die with our hearts clean."

When he uttered these words, the cheering stopped, and the crowd was silent. At first, I thought that my father had crushed their spirits, but I realized that thousands of them had taken his advice and were quietly praying.

In equipping these people, many of whom would die, with hope, my father was displaying warriorship—not of the earthly variety, but of the spiritual. After all, my father knew that we didn't stand a chance against our enemies. But the battle that would be waged was not an earthly one—it was one that was asking each and every one of us to challenge ourselves to walk in Jesus and Mary's footsteps . . . to enter into the sorrow and terror of our situation with faith, devotion, and an unwavering commitment to love . . . to stare the reality of sin and suffering directly in the eye and fearlessly meet its gaze.

## LESSON: BE WITH THE REALITY OF SIN AND SUFFERING

Not long ago, a friend of mine was going through a rough time. Her brother, who was her only family member who had survived the Rwandan genocide, was dying from a terminal illness. Through a haze of pain, she lamented, "It would be good if I could die before seeing him die."

There are times when our suffering can feel like too much to bear—and for many of us, it's even worse when we are faced with our loved ones' suffering. We don't always feel strong enough to remain present with the reality of what is happening, and to bring our full, loving, grounded attention to the moment. So often, when we are faced with the dark night of the soul and there seems to be no end in sight, our obstacles feel insurmountable, and the world can seem like a cruel and treacherous place; we just want to collapse onto the ground and give up.

Mary's Fifth Sorrow reminds us that even when we don't have the strength to continue, it is our willingness to remain present to the reality of sin and suffering that reveals to us a greater reality—that is, while we may be suffering now, we can choose to be spiritual warriors. We may not have weapons to fend off our enemies, but love itself becomes our defense. We are no longer willing to bury ourselves in the sand of denial and delusion. Rather, we meet life—full of its strange mixture of beauty and horror—with a clear gaze . . . even when it is painful, and even as tears of agony stream down our faces.

Mary has always encouraged her followers to allow their emotions to move through them rather than remaining numb, stoic, or seemingly unaffected. However, she also reminds us that these are fleeting moments. When we are strong enough to stand in our difficulties without averting our gaze or pretending that everything is fine, we discover that our presence has a transformative quality. Grace smiles down on us. God sees the way in which we are willing to courageously accept what life has given us. Instead of fighting the situation with weapons, we allow our love to be a bulwark against sin. Although we are not superhuman and many of us do not have the means to reverse injustice on this planet, it is our willingness to be present to the reality of sin and suffering that has the potential to change our lives. Like Mary, or my father, even if we do not have the resources to stand against sin, the most important resource we have is our capacity for presence, equanimity, faith, and love.

Think of Mary's strong presence throughout this ordeal. She had the grace and strength to remain with her son until the very end because she knew on some level that love always prevails over hatred. It can be difficult, sometimes, to accept that we were made in God's image when we look around and see so much that is wrong with the world: war, poverty, crime, natural disasters, and the epidemic of depression and loneliness that seems to ravage even those who are blessed with the resources to live well. But in truth, we don't have to look far to find God. Even when the world is crumbling around us, we can look within and find God in our own hearts.

As Mary stood before her dying son, I am sure that images of his life flashed before her eyes. She remembered the joy of watching him grow up, and she also remembered her anxiety and sorrow as she grappled with the prophecy that his life would be cut short someday. As these memories poured over her, threatening to engulf her, she remained by his side. As she was enduring what no mother should have to endure, it was God who made her strong at that moment. She must have known that her willingness to love even in the darkest times, in moments when it seemed that the world had no love to spare for her, was the only way.

This is what separates those who entrust themselves to God from those who allow their hearts to be hardened. The quiet but palpable voice of God is always here for us to access when we are willing to look within, to our hearts. After all, the root of the word *courage* is "cor," which is Latin for "heart." We display courage when we are willing to share what is in our heart. The heart is the seat of love, and it is always present, beckoning us back to the highest version of who we are.

When I was in hiding during the Rwandan genocide, Mary's Fifth Sorrow saved my life. I remember the experience of feeling like I had been literally transported to the cross on the day of Jesus's death. I could almost feel the dust that gathered on his brow and the blood that trickled down the wooden cross and gathered in a dark pool beneath him. I could see his face, made unrecognizable by injuries. I could also see that his mother, though alive, seemed to mirror her son's wretched condition, as her clothing was stained with dust, tears, and blood. Despite this, Mary's innate dignity and godliness could not be disguised. She didn't care what she looked like; she didn't care that she might have appeared to others as an abject being, degraded by virtue of the humiliation her son had to bear.

I considered the innocence of both Jesus and his Mother, who had never sinned. Jesus didn't deserve the punishment that was meted out to him; it was humanity that should have borne that burden. As I thought of Jesus and Mary, I realized that while I felt a closeness to them because of what I was going through, I was not so innocent. My pain became easier to endure. I was in a bathroom, safe at that moment, but I was not nailed to a cross or watching my child bear such degradation.

I remember the words of Jesus in his Sermon on the Mount. In Matthew 5:5, Jesus says, "Blessed are the meek, for they shall inherit the earth." Mary was an exemplar of the meekness that Jesus spoke about. Although we tend to equate meekness with weakness, this is not what Jesus meant. The quality of meekness is connected with quietude, thoughtfulness, and gentleness. A meek person does not want glory for themselves, but rather, they delight in the well-being of others. Moreover, the meek understand that God is always looking down upon us and judging the righteousness of our activity here on earth. Meekness is humility and selflessness; it is not pride or self-aggrandizement. The meek, like Mary, understand that even if we are unable to defeat our enemies, it is our willingness and our courage to stay present with our pain, and with those who need us, that will ultimately deliver us from sin and suffering.

Everybody hurts, and when we choose to open our awareness to the omnipresent reality of this pain, we ourselves are transfigured. We ourselves, like Mary, recognize that although this life might be brief and full of anguish, an eternity of love and peace awaits those who meet all the challenges of their lives with fortitude and a steady gaze.

## A Prayer for Working with Mary's Fifth Sorrow

*Dear Father, forgive us for our sins that caused your son to be tortured and executed. I am so sorry for my own sins, and the sins of the world. We are so grateful that you gave us the light of your love on the darkest day of all. You blessed us with the enormity of your love. You allowed yourself, in fleshly form, to undergo the most agonizing death for us, and in so doing, you opened the door to eternity and everlasting life. Thank you for the sacrifice you made. Please help us to love you with all our hearts so we may someday join you in heaven. Holy Mary, Mother of the Lord, just as you believed the angels' incredible message—that you would become the Mother of the Most High, so, too, you believed at the hour of his greatest abasement. In this way, at the hour of the cross, at the hour of the world's darkest night, you became the mother of all believers. You, who loved Our Lord so perfectly, teach us to love him too. I pray that all those who live without hope be blessed by the example of your unerring love and presence. On behalf of all those who are being persecuted by their enemies, those who are experiencing their final moment, please stand by their side as you stood there for Jesus; comfort them and lead them to your son, the Just Judge, and to eternal life. I beg you: teach us to believe in and be faithful to God, even in our suffering, and grant that our faith may bear fruit in courageous service and be the sign of a life ever ready to share suffering and to offer assistance. Amen.*

## Reflection Questions

Contemplate the Fifth Sorrow. Take some time to journal on or sit with the following inquiries.

1. Can you think of a time when your suffering transformed you? How did it change your perspective of yourself, life, and the world around you?

2. It is often said that it is darkest before the dawn. Have you experienced this firsthand in your life?

3. What does spiritual warriorship mean to you? How can you turn love into your strongest defense against sin and wickedness?

4. The next time you are faced with the brutal reality of human suffering and you are tempted to turn away, allow yourself to stay, tell God about the situation, pray, and help find an answer. Reflect on Mary's Fifth Sorrow and offer the prayer in this chapter. Notice how it makes you feel.

## CHAPTER 10

# THE SIXTH SORROW

### Mary Receives the Dead Body of Jesus

*Joseph of Arimathea, a noble counselor, came and went in boldly*
*to Pilate, and begged the body of Jesus. And Joseph buying fine linen,*
*and taking him down, wrapped him up in the fine linen.*

— MARK 15:43–46

As scripture shares with us, Jesus suffered on the cross for three hours before he finally breathed his last breath. These last moments of his life are an excruciating testament to his ability to always do his Father's will, even when it came at a great mental and physical cost—even when it required sacrifices beyond what most humans are capable of.

Many people misunderstand Jesus's entreaty to God, "Why have you forsaken me?" It is crucial for us to remember that though Jesus was a man, he was also the Son of God and God himself; he was simultaneously man and God incarnate. His words did not come from ego or insubordination; in fact, they demonstrated that although he was no ordinary human, he deeply understood the nature of human suffering, as well as the tendency to deny or push through suffering. Jesus demonstrated his willingness to be vulnerable and to open himself up to the spectrum of human emotions that accompany suffering. Despite all this, Jesus never begged his tormentors to release him, and nor did he capitulate to fear. He followed through with the tasks he had been given. He fulfilled the duties that his Father in Heaven had entrusted him with, well before he came into the world. He remained steadfast and endured through pain, temptation, and the darkest of human vices. When he asked his Father, "Why have you forsaken me?" in the time of his worst pain, he quickly caught himself and offered, "Not my will, but yours, be done." He showed us that although we might suffer and be tempted to give up, the most important thing we can do is catch ourselves so that we do not remain on the ground but rise up after falling.

What of Mary? Did Jesus's death bring her a sense of relief in the wake of witnessing him endure so much suffering? I am sure that in those fatal moments of receiving his body (which one of his disciples, Joseph of Arimathea, was able to retrieve after pleading with Pontius Pilate), Mary felt that she may as well have died with her son. Of all the sorrows, this is the one that brings the most tears to my eyes and makes me feel the sadness of Our Lady in the most palpable way.

I am reminded of the *Pietà*, the iconic sculpture by Renaissance artist Michelangelo, which is housed in St. Peter's Basilica in Vatican City. One of the greatest artistic masterpieces ever created, it perfectly captures the grief of a mother: Mary embraces the body of Jesus after his death. Her face is almost tranquil, almost as if she has wept all the tears she could possibly weep, and her devastation has given way to acceptance. As tragic as the scene is, it is imbued with a softness, a tenderness that underscores the sacred bond between mother and son. It is a highly idealized vision; despite the hours of torture and suffering, Michelangelo seems to be suggesting that there is no earthly action that can possibly desecrate Jesus or Mary.

While the sculpture offers a vision of Mary in deep reflection, I imagine that arriving at this seemingly serene place was not immediate. I am sure that it took Mary some time to get there. I can imagine Mary and John watching Jesus as he takes his final breath. I can imagine them staring in horror and grief at his lifeless body. The pain that Mary must have felt upon receiving Jesus's body likely became even more acute when Joseph of Arimathea brought him to her. In Jesus's time, Jewish burial customs entailed washing and anointing the loved one's body with expensive perfumes, such as myrrh and aloes. After this, the body is wrapped in a shroud, the face covered, and the hands and feet carefully bound with strips of cloth. Mary, as her son's next of kin, would have likely been responsible for preparing her son's body for burial. In fact, she shared with the visionary Marie-Claire that she washed Jesus's body with great care and reverence, to offer him her last respects: the dignity and love that were not accorded to him at the end of his life. She revealed that as she cleaned his bruised and bloodied body, she realized just how deep his wounds were, and how badly he had been hurt. She was aghast. How did he manage to carry the cross on his shoulders? How did he manage to walk at all? Mary told Marie-Claire that her only consolation was that Jesus was no longer being tortured. At the same time, recognizing the degree to which he had been so abused made her feel sick to her stomach. At that moment, she wished that she had died with him on the cross.

As she was washing his body, images of his life flashed before her eyes. She remembered the joy she'd felt when Angel Gabriel brought the good news, when she went to visit her cousin Elizabeth and the Holy Spirit moved her to sing the Magnificat. She remembered when he was born. She remembered her anxiety and sorrow as she grappled with the prophecy that his life would be cut short someday. She remembered him growing up, his first words, his first steps, when he became a teenager and an adult, the joy he brought her when he started to preach, the people he healed . . . and now he was lying in her hands, lifeless. As these memories poured over her, threatening to engulf her, she remained by his side, washing every wound carefully even as her own spirit was crushed.

## LAYING THE DEAD TO REST

Despite Mary's grief, her Sixth Sorrow reveals a powerful truth about the importance of honoring the dead and giving them the dignity they did not receive when they were alive. Rather than being left on the cross, Jesus's body is lovingly brought down by those who remain loyal to him. Sadly, so many people in our world are left to languish on their own crosses—crosses that are the consequence of war, hatred, persecution, addiction, and abandonment. Mary reminded Marie-Claire that everyone carries a cross, and we must carry our own with love. A poor man is worried about his poverty, and a rich man is worried about his wealth. But when we carry our crosses with Jesus by our side, in our hearts, meditating on his sorrows on earth, as well as Mary's sorrows, we find help in carrying our own.

Today, as I write this, I am painfully aware of the news coverage of the war in Ukraine, where so many people have been forced to leave behind the bodies of loved ones who became casualties in the midst of the cruelty and madness. In the aftermath of the genocide in my country, it was difficult to ignore the kind of injustice that leads to the death of innocent people. Although I had done my fair share of prayer and was committed to healing and forgiving, I knew that my heart and mind would always be tempted to feel anger—to find blame and hate. But I resolved that when the negative feelings came upon me, I wouldn't wait for them to grow or fester. I would always turn immediately to the Source of all true power: I would turn to God and let his love and forgiveness protect and save me.

After the United Nations peacekeepers came to Rwanda to help stabilize the country, I let one of the kind officers I met know that I still had aunts and an uncle living in my home province of Kibuye, although I hadn't seen them since the war. He was kind enough to fly me by helicopter to a soldiers' camp close to the village.

The next day we were preparing to leave for the five-mile hike to my village, when Captain Traore expressed concern about our safety. The genocide was over, but a palpable current of hostility ran through the country, and killing was still commonplace. The captain insisted on sending us with an armed escort, which consisted of no less than two dozen soldiers and five armored vehicles. We wouldn't be slinking into Mataba as returning refugees; instead, we'd enter with the pride of warriors. I had cowered too long in that village, and it felt good to go back with my head held high.

As we were driving, Psalm 91, which sustained me during the time of hiding, was playing in my heart like a song.

> *Whoever dwells in the shelter of the Most High will rest in the shadow of the Almighty.*
> *I will say of the Lord, "He is my refuge and my fortress, my God, in whom I trust."*
> *Surely he will save you from the fowler's snare and from the deadly pestilence.*
> *He will cover you with his feathers, and under his wings you will find refuge; his faithfulness will be your shield and rampart.*
> *You will not fear the terror of night, nor the arrow that flies by day,*
> *nor the pestilence that stalks in the darkness, nor the plague that destroys at midday.*
> *A thousand may fall at your side, 10,000 at your right hand, but it will not come near you.*
> *You will only observe with your eyes and see the punishment of the wicked.*
> *If you say, "The Lord is my refuge," and you make the Most High your dwelling,*
> *no harm will overtake you, no disaster will come near your tent.*
> *For he will command his angels concerning you to guard you in all your ways;*
> *they will lift you up in their hands, so that you will not strike your foot against a stone.*
> *You will tread on the lion and the cobra; you will trample the great lion and the serpent.*

*"Because he loves me," says the Lord, "I will rescue him;
I will protect him, for he acknowledges my name.
He will call on me, and I will answer him; I will be with
him in trouble, I will deliver him and honor him.
With long life I will satisfy him and show him my
salvation."*

I felt that the Lord was protecting me, that he had a plan for me. My mood quickly dissolved into sadness as we drove beneath the familiar sky of my childhood. I began weeping uncontrollably as we turned onto the road where my brothers and I had walked so often, then passed my mom's now-deserted schoolhouse, and rolled by the path we'd followed my dad along to go for our morning swims in Lake Kivu. I was inconsolable. I also saw shadowy faces peering at us through shuttered windows and closed gates . . . faces that belonged to the extremist Hutus who'd hunted and killed so many of my people. They owned the only houses still standing after they themselves had burned most of the Tutsi homes.

Finally, we reached my family's house. It was completely destroyed: no roof, no windows, no doors. A few partial walls stood watch over the scorched earth where we'd spent days listening to the radio while the killers prepared their massacre. I wandered through the stone skeleton, visiting the vacant rooms that had once formed my parents' dream home. There were no remnants of destroyed furniture or burnt clothing—our belongings had obviously been pilfered before the house was torched.

Several Hutus who had not partaken of the killings and a few of my surviving Tutsi neighbors saw our military escort and came out to greet me. They informed me of the grim events that had transpired while I was in hiding, telling me how my mother had been murdered and where her remains had been buried. Some of my brother Damascene's friends took me to the shallow grave where they'd hastily buried what was left of him. Karubu, our housekeeper, had witnessed my beloved brother's execution and gave me a word-for-word, blow-by-blow account.

The heartrending memories and the gory, gruesome details were all too much for me. I'd just begun to heal, and now I felt my wounds forced open again by the onslaught of brutal reality. I wanted to ask my neighbors and the soldiers to help me give my mother and brother a proper burial, but I couldn't speak. The lump growing in my throat stopped my voice, so I waved for the soldiers to take me back to the camp.

As we drove away from my home, past the unmarked mounds of dirt that covered Mom and Damascene, I felt the bitter, dirty taste of hatred in my mouth. On the return trip I looked at the faces peering at us as we passed, and I knew with all my heart that those people had blood on their hands—their neighbors' blood . . . my family's blood. I remembered many of those faces, who had watched us while we gathered around my father, before they killed us. I remembered how so many of them watched us die without offering help to hide any of us. Some were among the ones who had destroyed our house. As angry as I was, I realized how they had hurt themselves too. The village was empty, and their children were all alone, since their friends had been murdered. It felt like Jesus was reminding me that my family's killers didn't know what they had done; he was calling me to forgive them as he had forgiven his own killers. My feelings seemed to be shifting constantly, though—from understanding and forgiveness back to anger and disbelief. But ultimately, I was exhausted; I didn't want to harbor hatred and enmity toward any of them. I went straight to bed when we arrived at the camp without talking to anyone.

The next day, I asked the captain who was stationed at the camp if he'd take me back to the village so that I could properly lay my mother and brother, whom I knew had been killed, to rest. Most of the Tutsi genocide survivors in my village turned out, and a few Hutu friends joined us as well. One old family friend, Kayitare, brought two coffins with him, someone else brought a shovel and a Bible, and we all went together to recover the remains. First, we dug for Damascene; some neighbors crowded around me to block my view, gently pushing me back to protect me from seeing what was left of him.

I shoved past them. "He's my brother—I have to see him," I insisted.

I don't think I could ever have accepted that Damascene was really dead if I couldn't see his body with my own eyes. Then I heard the shovel scrape against bone, and I saw him . . . I saw his rib cage. The first thing I noticed was that he had no clothes on, and I remembered how they'd tried to strip him of his dignity before executing him.

"Don't look," someone said. But I had to—they'd chopped him up—his arms, his head. . . . *Oh, God, my sweet Damascene, what did they do to you?* I let out a kind of animal whimper. Someone bent down to the grave, then stood up and turned to me, holding my brother's skull in his hand. The jawbone was protruding, and then I saw the teeth . . . I recognized the teeth. All that remained of his beautiful smile was right there, staring up at me in a twisted, grotesque grin.

"Oh no . . . oh, Damascene . . . oh, blessed Mary, Mother of God!"

The earth rushed up at me, my head hit a stone, and then there was only blackness. I hadn't expected to faint, but when my mind at long last acknowledged my brother's death, it felt as if all the oxygen had been sucked out of the world. My relatives and neighbors revived me and lifted me to my feet, and we put Damascene's remains into a coffin and took it with us to find Mom. This time they insisted that I not look at the body, saying it was too decomposed and would be too upsetting. I acquiesced because I'd reached the limit of my pain. No matter how much I steeled my heart, the sight of my mother like that would have been too much for my eyes to bear. I agreed to bury her remains without seeing them. Instead, I'd remember her as she'd been in life . . . as she would forever stay in my heart and in my dreams.

As someone pounded nails into the lid of my mother's coffin, I looked at the faces of my friends and relatives—shattered faces reflecting shattered lives. There was my cousin, who'd been forced to watch her three boys slaughtered in front of her; my once-iron-willed Uncle Paul, who was now reduced to a shadow of his former self by the deaths of his beloved wife and seven children; and my aunts, whose husbands were dead and whose children were ill beyond recovery.

We all shared in the misery that had descended upon the village, but I knew that the people gathered around me had lost much more than I had. They'd lost their faith—and in doing so, they'd also lost hope. I stared at the coffins of my mother and Damascene and thought of my father and my brother Vianney, whose bodies I would never recover . . . and I thanked God. I may have lost everything, but I'd kept my faith, and it made me strong. It also comforted me and let me know that life still held purpose.

"Where shall we put them? Where shall we bury them?" Uncle Paul asked, sobbing as he ran his hands along the crude pine caskets.

"Home," I said. "We'll take them home and lay them to rest."

We carried the bodies of my mother and brother into the ruins of our home and dug a large grave in the center of one of the rooms where laughter and love had once echoed. There were no priests left in the village, so we performed the burial rites ourselves. I realized that everyone was looking to me to lead them into prayer, so I had to stop crying. Although no one was there to hold me in their arms and comfort me, I felt a strength I didn't realize I had. I started to offer some songs and prayers, and everyone followed. We sang some of my parents' favorite hymns and prayed many prayers. I asked God to hold my family close to him and watch over their beautiful souls in heaven . . . and just as Mary had with her beloved son, I said good-bye.

## LESSON: BE VULNERABLE AND LET YOURSELF GRIEVE

In all my travels across the world and back to my home country, I've met so many people who lived through similar grief and loss. For so many, the aftermath of their losses leaves them in a raw and vulnerable state. Some of them learn to harden their hearts and cover their tears with a show of strength and indifference;

others allow their vulnerability and grief to break their hearts open so they can receive the grace of God that surpasses their understanding, and find beauty and healing in this broken world.

Many of us are taught not to cry, to keep our feelings to ourselves, to feign strength and pretend that we're okay. In truth, as Mary has taught us, there is great power in allowing ourselves to be vulnerable . . . in allowing ourselves to grieve. Grief, ideally, is a state of being that brings us closer to one another and to God. We were not meant to be isolated in our suffering, which is exactly why Mary gave her sorrows to us—so that we might feel the depth of the pain that so many of us are taught to numb and deny.

It is little wonder that in places like Kibeho, where people have witnessed the atrocities of human violence firsthand, Mary's presence is palpable. So many people from my home country have found solace in Mary. She is a paragon of power—but it is not the kind of power we have come to see as power. It is a power that rests in openness, vulnerability, and acceptance . . . even of our grief.

Mary's vulnerability is clear throughout the Bible. She and her son did not live charmed or easy lives. They lived in poverty, in the midst of a brutal and unjust regime. For anyone who has ever experienced poverty, injustice, abuse, and brutal loss, Mary's Magnificat (Luke 1:46–55) is a powerful reminder that God recognizes our vulnerability and has the power to lift us up whenever we feel lost or insignificant. As Mary greets her cousin, Elizabeth, she is moved by the Holy Spirit and sings this song:

> And Mary said,
> "My soul magnifies the Lord,
> and my spirit rejoices in God my Savior,
> for God has looked with favor on the lowliness of the
>     Almighty's servant.
> Surely, from now on all generations will call me blessed;
> for the Mighty One has done great things for me,
> and holy is God's name.
> God's mercy is for those who fear God
> from generation to generation.
> God has shown strength with God's arm;

*God has scattered the proud in the thoughts of their
 hearts.
God has brought down the powerful from their thrones,
and lifted up the lowly;
God has filled the hungry with good things,
and sent the rich away empty.
God has helped his servant Israel,
in remembrance of God's mercy,
according to the promise God made to our ancestors,
to Abraham and to his descendants forever."*

The Magnificat is reminiscent of Jesus's proclamation that "the meek shall inherit the earth." It is a revolutionary depiction of the blessings that God will always bestow upon those of us who might feel beaten down by life—single parents, people burying family members caught in the crosshairs of violence, souls ravaged by poverty and hunger, neglected youth, lonely elders, and all those who have ever felt hopeless. As I myself have experienced, Mary sustains people in the midst of their raw pain and sorrow—but only if we are brave enough to open our hearts and express what is inside.

If anyone can understand the grief of the marginalized and disenfranchised, it is Our Mother Mary.

In too many traditions, Mary is depicted as an invisible, silent bystander. The truth couldn't be more different; there is nothing passive about the Blessed Virgin! It is her feminine strength and willingness to open herself to the full spectrum of her feelings that makes her a hallowed being. Moreover, although the New Testament primarily focuses on the teachings of Jesus, we must remember that Mary is like a beam of light shining down upon his good works. While Mary was the first disciple and apostle of her son, as he expressed to her all that he would teach to others, she was the one to teach and guide her son from birth, to take his first step, to say his first words. She supported him through all circumstances. She was there when he was betrayed, when so many who claimed to love him disappeared out of fear.

We can see from Mary's example that her status as a poor woman in ancient times made her extremely vulnerable—and so did her traditional femininity, which existed in a rich and textured emotional realm. And, of course, our feelings make us vulnerable, because it is such a taboo to reveal them in their entirety. After all, as I've mentioned, very few of us are taught that vulnerability is anything more than weakness. Children learn to suppress their feelings and to navigate the world of reason and logic (even though so many aspects of humanity are anything but reasonable or logical!).

But I insist that vulnerability is a gift. I believe that it is our willingness to deeply *feel* that bridges the gap between humans and God. I recall the words of C. S. Lewis:

> *To love at all is to be vulnerable. Love anything and your heart will be wrung and possibly broken. If you want to make sure of keeping it intact you must give it to no one, not even an animal. Wrap it carefully round with hobbies and little luxuries; avoid all entanglements. Lock it up safe in the casket or coffin of your selfishness. But in that casket, safe, dark, motionless, airless, it will change. It will not be broken; it will become unbreakable, impenetrable, irredeemable. To love is to be vulnerable.*

Much of what Jesus and Mary have taught us conflicts with the way we learn to survive in the world—as stoic creatures who create walls around our hearts in order to avoid hurt and pain. But anyone who has ever grieved (and that probably includes you, my dear reader) knows that while we can keep the pain at bay for a long time, we can't do so forever—and that suppressing grief and heartache also makes us less capable of fully receiving God's gifts. When we shut down our hearts, we lose our sense of connection to the world around us.

In a paradoxical way, Mary's vulnerability is tied to her courage. If we view vulnerability not as a weakness but as the capacity to fully receive what life is giving us, Mary displays this quality from the very beginning. She receives the message from Archangel

Gabriel; she receives Jesus as her beloved son; and she receives the reality of his death with heartfelt reverence and sorrow. Even in the midst of fear and pain, she does not deny the fullness of the bittersweet gift she has been given.

Mary is an example of what it means to place God at the center of our lives. When we do this, we relinquish control and surrender to a greater power than ourselves. We turn away from arrogance or the notion that we know what needs to happen. We turn away from immediate solutions and allow ourselves to experience the moment, exactly as it is. This is very difficult, as many of us have experienced. It is much easier to cling to self-righteousness or jump into action than it is to sit with our feelings, especially when they are soaked in grief.

Mary's Sixth Sorrow exemplifies the power of openness, receptivity, and vulnerability in the midst of our most heartbreaking experiences. If we cannot accept her as a being who is asking us to sit with the great mystery of life and death, we lose an important aspect of the message that Jesus brought to us—to enliven the word and will of God through our thoughts and deeds; to receive God's love with a jubilant "yes!" even when this causes others to turn against us; to meet evil with gentleness and divine fidelity.

Every time I reflect on how the Blessed Mother must have felt when she received the body of her son, I recognize that she offers us a vital lesson on what it means to confront our sorrow head-on. At the end of Jesus's life, she opens herself up to profound grief in such a way that there is no room for fear or rancor. And this, too, is what vulnerability offers us: the cleansing power of our tears, which allows us to move through difficult times with a pure heart.

After my experience burying my mother and brother, I knew that my family was at peace, but that didn't ease the pain of missing them. And I couldn't shake the crippling sorrow that seized my heart whenever I envisioned how they'd been killed. Every night, I prayed to be released from my private agony, from the nightmares that haunted my sleep and troubled my days. It took a while, but as always, God answered my prayers. This time, he did so by sending me a dream unlike any I've ever had, that brought me a comfort deeper than any I'd known before.

I had just discovered how my younger brother was killed that day, and I was very sad. I fell asleep crying. In my dream, I was on earth, and it was very dark. Around me were wet, broken trees and clumps of dirt, but I was standing in the light that came to me from the sky, which beamed down to me in a triangular shape, up from the endless heavens. The sky was very bright, almost as if I were peering into a clear diamond. I knew that this was the light of heaven. I could see my family in a line above me, as if they were posing for a family photograph.

Damascene took a few steps down toward me. He was wearing a crisp white shirt and blue trousers, while the rest of my family were dressed in white. My mother was dressed in traditional Rwandan clothes, her hair flowing in the wind. I could see that all of them were happy beyond words, as if they had great news to share.

Damascene came farther down, a few meters away from them, and looked at me with a joyful glow and his brilliant smile, so familiar to me. He said, "Look at where we are. I know you miss us, but would you wish for us to come back, or do you want to wait until you come to be with us?"

"No, no, Damascene!" I cried out, as tears of joy poured from my eyes. "Don't come back here! Wait for me there, and I will come join you all. When God is done with me in this life, I will come to you."

I felt so liberated from grief and gravity that I began to sing for joy. I sang from my heart, the words tumbling happily from my mouth. The song was "Mwami Shimirwa," which in Kinyarwanda means, "Thank you, God, for love that is beyond our understanding." As I was singing, the lady who was hosting me came and woke me: "You are singing so loud! Don't you know everyone is sleeping? Stop singing." I was upset that I'd been stirred from my beautiful dream, but I was also very happy.

From that night onward, my tears began to dry and my pain eased. I never again agonized over the fate of my family. I accepted that I would always mourn and miss them, but I'd never spend another moment worrying about the misery they'd endured. By sending me that dream, God had shown me that my family was in a place beyond suffering. And by sending me that dream, God brought me relief from the heaviest and darkest parts of my grief. Paradoxically, God showed me how tears of sorrow could become tears of joy; for in allowing our hearts to break, we leave space for God's grace to come rushing in.

I like to imagine that Mary went through something similar. Mary's vulnerability allowed her to grieve from the depths of her soul, to give herself over to the darkest nights in order to see that the light had always been there, waiting for her, reminding her that earthly sorrow will eventually fade . . . and after the storm, the sun shines brightly.

### A Prayer for Working with Mary's Sixth Sorrow

*Dear Father, thank you for the experience of this life, in which we get to live, love, and feel. We are imperfect humans who cling to our attachments as if they were permanent, but you are the only one with the power to grant everlasting life and heavenly joy. This is a world in which we live and die, in which we suffer and transform, and I pray that I learn to face all challenging moments with the grace and love of Jesus and Mary. I pray that instead of denying my experience or squashing my true feelings under false bravado or anger, I learn to fully mourn my losses so I can fill my cup with your blessings. I show you all those who suffer from silent grief, from unwept tears, from the abrupt loss of loved ones, from a heartache that cannot seem to be appeased. Thank you for giving us Mother Mary, whose forbearance and gentleness help us to share the contents of our hearts with you, so that you can offer us your healing grace. Amen.*

## Reflection Questions

Contemplate the Sixth Sorrow. Take some time to journal on or sit with the following inquiries.

1. Think of your relationship to grief. Do you fear or welcome grief? Do you let yourself grieve fully, or do you push your pain aside to "get on with" life? Find a loved one, or a good friend to share your heart with; if not, speak to Mary. She listens. Open your heart and share your pain with someone who understands it.

2. Think of your relationship to vulnerability. Is it difficult or easy for you to be vulnerable? Were you raised to view vulnerability as a weakness? Can you see the strength that exists within vulnerability?

3. Often, God's grace accompanies experiences of profound heartbreak. When have you most strongly felt the presence of God's grace? Has it ever whispered in your ear when you felt bereft?

4. The next time you experience difficult feelings, especially those connected to grief and heartbreak, notice the fear-based defenses that keep you from fully allowing these feelings to pierce your heart, or that make you want to hide. Instead of hiding, allow yourself to express your feelings to God, or to Mary in your privacy; you are never alone, they are your constant help and friends. Wail, cry, stomp, write about it. Welcome your feelings as a gift. Reflect on Mary's Sixth Sorrow and offer the prayer in this chapter. Notice how it makes you feel.

## CHAPTER 11

# THE SEVENTH SORROW

## Jesus in the Tomb

*Now there was in the place where he was crucified, a garden; and in the garden a new sepulchre, wherein no man yet had been laid. There, therefore, because of the parasceve of the Jews, they laid Jesus, because the sepulchre was nigh at hand.*

— JOHN 19:41–42

The day of preparation for Jesus's body was the day before Sabbath. As you already know, this was when Joseph of Arimathea, a disciple of Jesus, courageously requested that Pontius Pilate offer the body of Jesus to his family and beloved followers. Apparently, Pilate expressed surprise that Jesus was already dead, as he didn't expect it to happen quite so quickly. Perhaps in burying his head in the sand he expected that the situation would calm down and that the mob of people who had called so virulently for Jesus's death would eventually be appeased. Pilate accepted Joseph's request.

After Mary lovingly prepared her son's body and anointed him with fragrant perfumes, Jesus was wrapped in a linen cloth and laid to rest in a tomb that had been carved out from the rock of a cave. At this point, it is believed that Joseph rolled a stone against the entrance to the tomb. While it must have been a somber time, we know that Jesus resurrected and came back to life three days after he was crucified.

There is a finality to this moment in time that is important to consider as we ponder the Seven Sorrows Rosary. By this point, Mary has experienced the uncertainty, vulnerability, profound joy, and deep sorrow of being the Mother of God. When we come to the interment of Jesus's body into the tomb, we consider the scope of everything that Mary has experienced over the course of her son's 33 years.

When Mary appeared to Marie-Claire in Kibeho, Rwanda, she taught her the Seven Sorrows, including the order of prayers and what they are about. After a little time, Marie-Claire was able to recite the Seven Sorrows Rosary by heart. During one of her visions, Marie-Claire was asked by Mary if she knew how to say the rosary well. Marie-Claire responded, "Yes, I know it by heart." Mary's response surprised her: "No, my child, you don't know the rosary well. In order to say it well, you have to meditate on the sorrows and put yourself in my place as you pray, and ask yourself what I felt and what you would feel if it had been you."

Marie-Claire realized that she needed to spend more time thinking and meditating on each of the Seven Sorrows—specifically on what Mary had been through as Jesus's mother. The more Marie-Claire thought about what Mary had felt, the more her heart broke. Her sorrow commingled with Mary's, which made her feel even more loved by and closer to Mary.

So, this final sorrow is an opportunity for those praying the rosary to truly ask themselves: *What would I have felt had this been me? What might I have experienced as Jesus was being placed in the tomb? If I were Mary, the person who loved Our Lord the most, what would be the flavor of my grief? Can I allow myself to let such grief into my heart?*

It can be overwhelming to put ourselves in Mary's shoes. Mary was at the burial of Jesus on Good Friday, the same day her son died. Hours before, she had been beside him at the cross; she had trekked with him toward Calvary, where he was crucified. She was there, sitting with the sinking realization that Jesus was willingly sacrificing himself, despite the fact that he had a power far greater than that of Pilate, the Pharisees, or the Roman Empire. Before this, she was there when Pilate condemned Jesus and released the bandit Barabbas when the angry crowd insisted that he be chosen over Jesus in a customary pardon of a criminal before the feast of Passover.

The details of the hours leading up to her son's death must have been overwhelming. Mary must have been sitting with a chaotic range of emotions, from inconsolable grief to the recognition that her son had given himself up for the love of all of humanity. Although he had submitted himself to a punishment he did not deserve, his death would soon give way to his resurrection . . . and with that, to the promise of eternal life for all those who followed his path and walked in his footsteps.

It is not a far cry for me to imagine Mary's plight, as well as the choices she faced: to accept her son's death and mourn his loss with all the love in her heart—or to find a way to exact revenge on all those who had consigned him to such a miserable fate.

I recall the time when I discovered my brother Damascene's body, and the unceremonious way in which he had been left on the street to rot. I went through a great deal of suffering, but because the suffering was so unbearable and almost too intense for me to hold, I have found myself more openly mourning that loss as I pray with the Seven Sorrows. I think of how my awareness of every moment leading up to Damascene's death pulls at a unique part of my heart. When I first learned that he had been killed, I felt lost and didn't know how I would be able to feel joy again. I was shaken to my core. I didn't know how I would navigate a world that no longer had my strong, kind brother in it. And then, when I discovered the nature of his death, it was a different pain . . . and my previous suffering was renewed. This continued to happen as I discovered more details about his death, such as how he'd been killed in public after verbally defending himself rather than standing down. Everyone I spoke to about Damascene's death had a different story to share that opened up the wounds I'd mistakenly believed had healed into scars. Eventually I had to stop inquiring about it, because it only hurt me more. I had to realize that Damascene was gone, and he would never come back again. Finally, when I buried him, the unique pain of facing this reality made me feel that I would never function again. I still recall the desire to be buried alongside him, to keep him company . . . as if that would change anything. When we placed his bones into the earth, I could feel my stomach churning and my intestines burning; it was an inexplicable pain that I'd never felt before and hope never to feel again.

On several occasions, I experienced my world ending. This is why I feel so connected to Mary's Seventh Sorrow. By this time, her parents are dead; her husband is dead; and now, her son, her only child, is dead. Mary told Marie-Claire that when they buried Jesus, her new source of suffering was the loneliness she felt. She lived to care for Jesus, who was the object of her affection. But despite the fact that Mary's life, her reason to live, seemed like it had been extinguished like the flame of a candle, she understood that she was in God's hands . . . and it was up to him to decide her new path in life.

As I have mentioned before, scripture tells us that Mary never sinned, not even once, in her life. When her son was murdered, she suffered, but not once did she direct anger or thoughts of vengeance at Jesus's killers. She did not engage in spiritual bypassing (that is, using "spiritual" explanations to deny or avoid difficult feelings), but she also understood that everyone has their own unique path in life, and that it is up to God, not us, to judge. Thus, Mary is a beautiful model, a glowing example, for how we might conduct ourselves in this life: without gall, bitterness, or blazing anger that we weaponize by choosing to direct it outward.

I recall the moments I have dialogued with Jesus to understand why he made the decision he made. I have asked, "Why did you have to go through this suffering, this torture? Couldn't you have simply done it from heaven?"

The response I received filled my soul: "Because I loved you, I did it this way. I wanted not only to save you with words, but through action. I wanted to show you that if you go through anything close to this—remember, I was there before you. If you are ever rejected, if you are ever not well loved, remember, I was there before you. So, learn from me. Look at what they did to me. But don't hate. Forgive as I did. Control yourself, and let God's will be done in you."

It was not easy to hear, but Jesus's words, as well as my contemplations on Mary, are what eventually led me to forgive . . . to let go of the anger I harbored in my heart toward the perpetrators of the genocide. I wanted to do God's will, as he was my only support, and nothing else seemed to work or be trustworthy. I would always strive to remember his words on the cross: "Forgive them, Father, for they know not what they do." Although it wasn't easy and I had to recall the examples set by Jesus and Mary countless times, I knew that the only way I would be able to reach paradise that Our Lord promised to us was through forgiveness. I wanted to walk in the path of Jesus and Mary. And when I did, it freed me.

## FROM VICTIM TO VICTOR: THE PATH OF FORGIVENESS

I still vividly remember the moment when I understood that forgiveness is an antidote to the hatred and fear we might carry in our hearts when we experience suffering and injustice. During the genocide, as I was hiding in the pastor's home, one night I heard screaming not far from the house, and then a baby crying. I realized in horror that the killers must have slain the mother and left her infant to die in the road. The child wailed all night; by morning, its cries were feeble and sporadic, and by nightfall, it was silent. I heard dogs snarling nearby and shivered as I thought about how that baby's life had ended. I prayed for God to receive the child's innocent soul, and then I asked him, *How can I forgive people who would do such a thing to an infant?*

I heard his answer as clearly as if we'd been sitting in the same room chatting: "You are all my children . . . and the baby is with me now." It was such a simple sentence, but it was the answer to the prayers I'd been lost in for days.

The killers were like children. Yes, they were barbaric creatures who would have to be held accountable for their actions, but they were still children. They were cruel, vicious, and dangerous, as kids can sometimes be, but nevertheless, they were children. They saw, but didn't understand, the terrible harm they'd inflicted. They'd blindly hurt others without thinking. They'd hurt their Tutsi brothers and sisters. They'd hurt God—and they didn't understand how badly they were hurting themselves. Their minds had been infected with the evil that had spread across the country, but their souls weren't evil.

Despite their atrocities, they were still children of God, and I could forgive a child, although it would not be easy—especially when that child was trying to kill me. In God's eyes, the killers were part of his family, deserving of love and forgiveness. I knew that I couldn't ask God to love me if I were unwilling to love his children.

At that moment, I prayed for the killers, for their sins to be forgiven. I prayed that God would lead them to recognize the horrific error of their ways before their life on earth ended—before they were called to account for their mortal sins. I held on to the rosary my father had given me before we'd been separated, and I asked God to help me, and again I heard his voice: "Forgive them, Father, for they know not what they do." I took a crucial step toward forgiving the killers that day. My anger was draining from me. I'd opened my heart to God, and he'd touched it with his infinite love. For the first time, I pitied the killers. I asked God to forgive their sins and turn their souls toward his beautiful light.

That night, I prayed with a clear conscience and a clean heart. For the first time since I entered the bathroom, I slept in peace. But later, when my neighbors whispered the stories of my family's sadistic murders in my ear, the feelings of hatred that I thought I'd banished from my soul sprang violently from the depths of my being with renewed vigor. I tossed and turned for hours. I knew the devil was tempting me—that he was leading me away from the light of God, from the freedom of his forgiveness. I could feel the weight of my negative thoughts dragging me away from the one light that had guided me through the darkness. I never felt lonelier than I did that night. God was my truest friend, and these feelings were a wall between us. I knew that my thoughts caused him pain, and that knowledge tortured me. I rolled out of bed and got down on my knees.

"Forgive my evil thoughts, God," I prayed. "Please . . . as you always have, take this pain from me and cleanse my heart. Fill me with the power of your love and forgiveness. Those who did these horrible things are still your children, so let me help them, and help me to forgive them. Oh, God, help me to love them."

It would take me many tries to feel this forgiveness at the core of my being. Some time after burying Mom and Damascene, I knelt by their graves and told them all that had happened since I'd last seen them. I told them about my job at the U.N., which I'd secured after the genocide, and what I planned to do in the future. I missed seeing their faces and hearing their voices, and I wept. But this time, my tears were a release, not a sorrow.

And then, it was time to do what I'd come to do.

I still remember the day I experienced the full power of forgiveness. I arrived at the prison late in the afternoon and was greeted by Semana, the new burgomaster (mayor) of Kibuye province, where my family had lived. Semana had been a teacher before the genocide, as well as a colleague and good friend of my dad's—he was like an uncle to me. Four of his six children had been killed in the slaughter, and I told him he must have faith that his little ones were with God.

"I can see how much the world has changed; the children now comfort the parents," he replied sadly.

As burgomaster, Semana was a powerful politician in charge of arresting and detaining the killers who had terrorized our area. He'd interrogated hundreds of Interahamwe and knew better than anyone which killers had murdered whom. And he knew why I'd come to see him. "Do you want to meet the leader of the gang that killed your mother and Damascene?"

"Yes, sir, I do."

I watched through Semana's office window as he crossed a courtyard to the prison cell and then returned, shoving a disheveled, limping old man in front of him. I jumped up with a start as they approached, recognizing the man instantly. His name was Felicien, and he was a successful Hutu businessman whose children I'd played with in primary school. He'd been a tall, handsome man who always wore expensive suits and had impeccable manners. I shivered, remembering that it had been his voice I'd heard calling out my name when the killers searched for me at the pastor's. Felicien, who had known me, had specifically hunted me.

Semana pushed Felicien into the office, and he stumbled onto his knees. When he looked up from the floor and saw that I was the one who was waiting for him, the color drained from his face. He quickly shifted his gaze and stared at the floor.

"Stand up, killer!" Semana shouted. "Stand up and explain to this girl why her family is dead. Explain to her why you murdered her mother and butchered her brother. Get up, I said! Get up and tell her!"

Semana screamed even louder, but the battered man remained hunched and kneeling, too embarrassed to stand and face me. His dirty clothing hung from his emaciated frame in tatters. His skin was sallow, bruised, and broken; and his eyes were filmy and crusted. His once-handsome face was hidden beneath a filthy, matted beard; and his bare feet were covered in open, running sores. I wept at the sight of his suffering. Felicien had let the devil enter his heart, and the evil had ruined his life like a cancer in his soul. He was now the victim of his victims, destined to live in torment and regret.

I was overwhelmed with pity for the man.

"He looted your parents' home and robbed your family's plantation, Immaculée. We found your dad's farm machinery at his house, didn't we?" Semana yelled at Felicien. "After he killed Rose and Damascene, he kept looking for you . . . he wanted you dead so he could take over your property. Didn't you, pig?" Semana shouted again.

I flinched, letting out an involuntary gasp. Semana looked at me, stunned by my reaction and confused by the tears streaming down my face. He grabbed Felicien by the shirt collar and hauled him to his feet. "What do you have to say to her? What do you have to say to Immaculée?"

Felicien was sobbing. He didn't have to say anything; I could feel his shame. He looked up at me for only a moment, but our eyes met. I reached out, touched his hands lightly, and quietly said what I'd come to say: "I forgive you."

My heart eased immediately, and I saw the tension release in Felicien's shoulders before Semana pushed him out the door and into the courtyard. Two soldiers yanked Felicien up by his armpits and dragged him back toward his cell. When Semana returned, he was furious.

"What was that all about, Immaculée? That was the man who murdered your family. I brought him to you to question . . . to spit on if you wanted to. But you forgave him! How could you do that? Why did you forgive him?"

I answered him with the truth: "Forgiveness is all I have to offer."

And it was absolutely true. I know now what Mary might have known in the wake of Jesus's death: God saved my soul and spared my life for a reason. He left me to tell my story to others and show as many people as possible the healing power of his love and forgiveness.

## LESSON: LIVE THE GIFTS OF GOD'S FORGIVENESS AND LOVE

God's message extends beyond borders: anyone in the world can learn to forgive those who have injured them, however great or small that injury may be. I see the truth of this every day. For example, once when I shared my story with a new friend, a few days later she called to say that my experiences had inspired her to contact an uncle she'd been close to but hadn't spoken to in seven years. "We'd had a big fight, and I was so angry that I swore I'd never speak to him again," she confided. "But after hearing how you managed to forgive the people who killed your family, I had to pick up the phone and call him. I didn't ask him for an apology—I just opened my heart and forgave him. Soon we were talking the way we used to, with so much love. We couldn't believe that we'd wasted so many years."

Similarly, a genocide survivor whose family had been murdered called me from Rwanda, crying over the phone and asking me to explain the steps I'd taken to forgive my family's killers. "I thought you were crazy to forgive them, Immaculée, that you were letting them off the hook. But the pain and bitterness I've been carrying in my heart for eleven years is about to kill me. I've been so miserable for so long that I don't have the energy to live anymore. But I keep hearing people talk about how you forgave your family's killers and moved on with your life . . . that you're happy and have a husband, children, and a career! I need to learn how to let go of my hatred too. I need to live again."

Then, there was the woman in Atlanta, Georgia, who approached me in tears at the end of a talk I gave. She told me that her parents had been killed in the Nazi Holocaust when she was a baby: "My heart has been full of anger my entire life . . . I've suffered and cried over my parents for so many years. But hearing your story about what you lived through and were able to forgive has inspired me. I've been trying all my life to forgive the people who killed my parents, and now I think I can do it. I can let go of my anger and be happy."

On so many occasions, I've heard such stories from people, ranging from tales of estrangement from a family member to tragic accounts of all that was lost in times of war and separation. Over and over, I've heard people marvel at the idea of forgiveness, because they took for granted that it was too late for them, that their hearts had already grown too cold and armored to ever entertain the possibility. However, I know without a doubt that forgiveness, like the love of God, is always available to us. It is the healing balm that can turn a wounded, breaking heart into a heart that is large enough to hold both the joy and suffering of the world.

The love of a single heart can make a world of difference. I believe this is what Mary intended to show us . . . on all the occasions when she appeared to humble, unsuspecting people to reveal the power of God's miracles . . . and when she revealed herself and her sorrows to the world as a guide for how we can live with and transform our suffering into purpose. Moreover, I am reminded that no matter how dire the situation at hand might seem, we can always choose love and discover ourselves anew through it. After all, Jesus resurrected three days after he was placed in the tomb, proving that, indeed, he had the power to make all things new. It is this promise of newness, of restoration after any long period of hardship, that convinces me it is possible to heal our world—by healing one heart at a time.

I know that forgiveness is one of the fastest routes to healing. Aside from freeing us from the burden of hatred, which increases our suffering a thousandfold, it helps us to recognize that our suffering is never in vain. It is my suffering and my losses that have led me to the most wonderful life imaginable—one in which I get to share my story with others and inspire them to harness the strength and love of God in the most troubling of circumstances. It is my suffering and my losses that have opened my heart and mind to the possibility of redemption and forgiveness. It is my suffering and my losses that have helped me to cultivate a close relationship with both Jesus and Mary, who I know are always watching over me.

Christians experience the metaphorical power of transubstantiation through the eucharistic prayer, when the substance of bread is transmuted into the body of Christ and wine becomes his blood. The Eucharist is a mystery we are all invited to step into. Through it, we receive God's heavenly food and allow it to transform us so that, ideally, we experience what it means to live as Jesus Christ . . . to be the blessed beneficiaries of his sacrifice.

We transform unequivocally when we come to realize that we are so much more than our flesh, our bodily impulses, our instincts toward greed and anger. I believe that we live under the control of the flesh when we act out of integrity with our spirit, when we give in to the basest of our desires. In contrast, forgiveness is a virtue of the soul that we can all learn to embrace; and the more we do it, with the utmost sincerity, with the awareness that those who sin have created a hell for themselves without knowing it, we ourselves are transformed.

Up until his final hours on earth, Jesus demonstrated the power of forgiveness, as it is taught to us through the Lord's Prayer: "Forgive us our trespasses, as we forgive those who trespass against us" (Matthew 6:12). When Peter asks how many times we should forgive another, Jesus replies, "Seventy times seven" (Matthew 18:21–22). Throughout the Bible, we see so many examples of Jesus's forgiveness toward others. During the Last Supper, he informs his apostles to drink from the cup, "for this is my blood of the covenant, which is poured out for many for the forgiveness of sins" (Matthew 26:27–28). Even after his resurrection, he enjoins his disciples to forgive: "Receive the Holy Spirit. If you forgive the sins of any, they are forgiven; if you retain the sins of any, they are retained" (John 20:22–23).

So even if it takes us seventy times seven times to forgive someone who has wronged us, the willingness to keep returning to forgiveness, just as our Heavenly Father consistently forgives us, opens our heart to divine generosity. Just as we accept God's forgiveness, we too learn to forgive others.

I want to clarify something important here: I am not suggesting that when you forgive, you also forget or act naively. I believe in the power of accountability, especially when a person's crimes include crimes against humanity, as Felicien's did. Just because I forgave Felicien didn't mean that he suddenly became my best friend—or even that he changed. I knew that if he'd gotten a chance, he would very likely have killed me. It is important to be wise, to recognize your boundaries, and to honor them when it comes to making the decision of whether or not to let someone who has wronged you back into your life in a more intimate way. I have certainly heard cases of individuals whose family members were murdered who go on to forgive the killer—to the extent that they form a lasting connection with that person. I know some people who killed my family members and who truly repented, who apologized with deep regret for what they had done. I am still in touch with those people; with some of them, I am even friendly. I am not suggesting that you do this, but I do know that when you open your heart to God's will for you, it will become easier to make the right decision. Everyone's forgiveness journey is their own. However, I advise you never to wait for anyone else to apologize or to extend your forgiveness. Forgiveness is your gift to give.

What I want to stress is that forgiveness frees us from the straitjacket of unchecked anger and hatred. It is just as much for ourselves as it is for other people. When we give our precious life energy over to hatred or revenge, we find that we are still at the mercy of what has been done to us. Our every action revolves around the terrible things that happened to us, rather than what we have chosen to make of those unfortunate circumstances. The person or people who wronged us continue to wield control over us, as we succumb to self-pity or obsessive thoughts about "payback." We deserve to create a present and future that are free from needless suffering and that are worthy of God's will for us. But we cannot do so if we are still shackled to the past in ways that cause us to persist in our victimhood.

The wonderful thing about forgiveness is that you need not ever have contact with the person you are forgiving in order to reap its benefits. Let's take Mary as an example. We know that three days after his crucifixion, Jesus resurrects from the dead and brings his glorious salvation to everyone. Mary didn't know this would happen, but after burying her son, instead of dwelling on making the ones who persecuted Jesus pay for their crimes, she focuses her time and energy on comforting his followers and going about her business with the utmost humility, even in the midst of her own sadness.

I believe that when we do not allow ourselves to fully grieve, to fully express the depth of our emotions and sorrow, as Mary did, those emotions stagnate and fester, and we either use them to harm ourselves or to harm others. This is why the Seven Sorrows constitute such a powerful prayer. It helps us to get to the heart of our grief—for below anger, hatred, fear, frustration, numbness . . . there is usually a well of grief whose depths we have not touched. When we go down to that well, with Mary by our side, we realize that in many ways we are a world that is full of unwept tears and unmourned losses, and we cannot help but wish for others the same tenderness we feel for ourselves, Our Lady, and Our Lord.

Let Mary's innate dignity, emotional honesty, and goodness always serve to sustain you through your most difficult trials. When you feel tempted to sin against someone who wronged you, remember Mary. Perhaps, at some point, you'll realize there is no need to forgive at all—because you never harbored any ill will toward another to begin with. Like Mary, you will have chosen to live in the light of God's grace, knowing that he is the ultimate judge, and that in healing your heart of any malice or ill intent you contribute to the healing of our world.

### A Prayer for Working with Mary's Seventh Sorrow

Dear Father, thank you for giving us Mary to be our mother and our model. We are so grateful that you brought her to us, that you showed your strength in her, as she never separated herself from you, even when she was brokenhearted. I beg you to please hear our prayers, as we are still here in the valley of tears. I beg you to listen to her prayers, as she prays for us, the children you gave her through your son, Jesus. Dear Father, I offer to you those who are lost or killed, and their loved ones who are grieving bitterly. Please open their hearts to your grace so that they may live in your love and forgiveness. I offer you those who are lonely and have few family or friends—please be their friends and their support. I offer you the souls in purgatory. I offer you the whole world that they may come to know the one who has saved them and accept their loving Mother Mary, who intercedes for them. Help us to know her role in our salvation, and to love her, just as we love you. Amen.

## Reflection Questions

Contemplate the Seventh Sorrow. Take some time to journal on or sit with the following inquiries.

1.  Is there someone you have not yet forgiven, or a grudge you are continuing to hold? What is the cost of holding on? What has the impact been on your life and your access to joy?

2.  Forgiveness is not just for others, but also for ourselves. Is there something you have yet to forgive yourself for? Remembering God's love for all of us, how can you be receptive to self-forgiveness?

3.  Often, when we are holding on to a grudge, it is because we have not allowed ourselves to fully feel our feelings, including our grief. Is there something in your life that still needs to be grieved? Ask Mary to hold your hands and hear you; do not be afraid.

4.  Forgiving is not the same as forgetting. Can you think of ways in which forgiveness and accountability can go hand in hand?

5.  The next time you harbor a hateful or vengeful thought toward someone else, consider how you can approach them with forgiveness (and this includes you, if you are holding punitive thoughts toward yourself). If you cannot sincerely forgive that person, pray that God, in his infinite goodness and mercy, will act as an example for you. Reflect on Mary's Seventh Sorrow and offer the prayer in this chapter. Notice how it makes you feel.

# PART III

# "OUR HEARTS HAVE BEEN TOUCHED"

*The Rewards of Devotion*

## CHAPTER 12

# THE MIRACLES OF THE SEVEN SORROWS

*I have come to prepare the way for him for your own good*
*and yet you don't want to accept, you do not want to understand.*
*There is so little time remaining, and yet you still allow yourself to*
*be distracted by earthly goods and desires, which will soon pass*
*away. I see so many of my children going astray, and so I come*
*to plead with them and show them the correct way.*

— OUR LADY OF KIBEHO

There is something about going back to my home country of Rwanda, where I lead pilgrimages for people three times a year, that takes my breath away and breaks my heart open. While Rwanda has been memorialized as the site of one of the greatest tragedies of the 20th century, I will always see it as a place where people live simply but with such a generosity of spirit that it shines through in their smiles and their friendly curiosity toward visitors from across the world.

Rwanda has been called the "land of a thousand hills," but this doesn't do its natural beauty justice. Every time I fly into Kigali International Airport, I am awestruck by the rolling greenery spread out below me like a vision of paradise. Long, sparkling rivers flow through the mountains, creating a terrain that is both ethereal and welcoming. Sometimes, even from that distance, I can imagine myself on the calm turquoise waters of Lake Kivu, catching a strain of song from the well-known "singing fishermen" who greet the evening with their soulful music.

I often whisper to myself as I look down on the land, dotted with slushy rice fields, verdant tea plantations, and towering canopies of rain forest: "I'm home, at last."

It is a bittersweet feeling, because the beauty of this place is matched by the suffering that the land has borne witness to. And there is nowhere in Rwanda where this mixture of beauty and suffering feels quite as apparent as it does in the small southwestern town of Kibeho.

## THE ROAD TO KIBEHO

Kibeho is a place whose medicine continues to percolate in people's lives for years to come. And despite the fact that I've been going to Kibeho since I was very young, it always brings up a feeling of newness and anticipation in me every time I visit. As the bus jostles along the bumpy (and often muddy, given that the verdant land is the result of heavy rainfall throughout the year) road to Kibeho, my heart soars. As the elevation changes, there is a palpable sense of reverence. Even the air seems sweeter. As we approach, I see the beautiful statue of Mary in her white dress and sky-blue veil; the creators of the statue made it so that Our Lady appears to be floating above an aureole of flowers. Upon seeing her, I know that I'm exactly where I need to be . . . in a place of unbounded hope and miracles . . . a place that has transformed the tragedy of the genocide into the grace of a new beginning.

I will always remember my final visit to Kibeho before I moved to the United States with my husband, Bryan. I was fortunate to meet Bryan shortly after the genocide, as he had come to Rwanda to help set up the International Criminal Tribunal, the United

Nations court that prosecuted those who'd been responsible for planning the genocide. As soon as I met him, I realized he matched the image of the husband I always knew I would have: kind, brave, strong, and devoted to God. Two years after our meeting, we were married in a traditional Rwandan ceremony.

In 1998, I was pregnant with my daughter, Nikeisha. At this time, Bryan and I decided that we would move to the U.S. permanently. While I was excited to begin a new life in a new country with my family, I knew that I could not leave Rwanda without making a trip to Kibeho, the site of the Shrine of Our Lady of Sorrows. Because the road to Kibeho was long and potentially dangerous, it can take three to four hours to get from the main area of Kigali to Kibeho, depending on the road and weather conditions. My doctor informed me that it would be very risky to make the trek to Kibeho while I was pregnant, and he advised me not to go. Despite this warning, I felt that I had no choice. I needed to secure Mary's blessings from this holy site before I found myself in a completely new country, out of my element. While I didn't want to lie to my husband, I recognized that there was no way he'd agree to my plan, as he would be too worried about my well-being and the safety of our unborn daughter.

I should say that I was not purposely attempting to disobey my doctor or husband and put myself in harm's way. I knew in my heart that I would be all right; as long as I was going to Kibeho for my Mother Mary, she would protect me. I had lived too extraordinary a life and had seen too many miracles to chalk them up to mere coincidence. I had already experienced my own miracles by going to Kibeho. When I was a college student, I decided to leave school when I should have been studying for an exam so that I could pay a visit to the place where the Marian apparitions had occurred. Since I didn't have time to study, I picked out 10 random pages from my textbook to peruse before the exam. Remarkably, the entire exam came from those 10 pages I'd read! I knew this was a direct message from Mary, who seemed to be showing me that my devotion to her and to God would reap rewards I couldn't possibly imagine.

My experiences had taught me that those who give themselves heart and soul to Our Lady will always be blessed by her protection and care. Such people need only to be sure that their intentions are righteous and their love authentic—because the Mother of God can see right through us to the core of our true intentions.

The day I made my final trip to Kibeho before my big international move, my husband drove me to work at 7 A.M. and we said our good-byes. But instead of heading into the building, I promptly boarded the bus to Kibeho. Although the drive was mostly smooth, at one point the passengers were asked to get out of the bus to help push it out of a mud puddle in which it had become stuck. All the while, I continued to pray silently. I knew that Mary had to be close at hand, and that she was gently standing watch over me, ensuring that I would be safely delivered to my destination—and then back home.

My time at the Shrine of Our Lady of Sorrows was precious and powerful. I still remember myself kneeling in the chapel, praying to Our Lady to ensure that the move to the U.S. would be easeful and auspicious . . . that my family would find a welcoming home in which we could continue to grow and flourish under God's loving gaze. Although I was mostly excited about the move, I was also somewhat anxious, as I had no friends or family awaiting me in the U.S. And although I knew I would be going to a place with greater opportunities, some part of me ached at the thought of leaving Rwanda, which is a poor country that is overflowing with abundant natural beauty and a kindness and simplicity that had not been quashed by the genocide. "I give all of these worries to you, Mother," I whispered quietly. "I dedicate this journey to you, and I trust you to guide me in this new adventure."

Although I was only in the chapel for 30 minutes or so, my heart was at peace as I headed back down to Kigali on the bus, which took another four hours. Of course, given the length of the journey, my husband was already waiting for me by the time I returned to my workplace. Not to mention, I was covered in mud after the ordeal of pushing the bus out of the puddle. My husband looked at me, mouth agape, and asked, "What happened to you?"

Of course, I had no choice but to admit I'd taken the day off so I could go to Kibeho to pray. Predictably, he was very upset. In his mind, I'd been reckless and had unnecessarily endangered myself and our unborn daughter. Thankfully, I was already prepared.

"I'm very sorry for causing you to worry, but the reason I didn't tell you about it is that I knew you would never say yes to my going. I must explain to you that I have my life with God, which no one can ever take from me. You might not always be happy with the decisions I make, but you have to understand that they come directly from my relationship with God, which always takes priority over everything else. That's why you fell in love with me! You have to accept that because Mary and Jesus will come first, they will always be here to protect me, and us. And while I understand that you love me and want me to be safe, it is ultimately only Mary and Jesus who have the power to protect me—and they always will."

What could Bryan do? He was just glad that I was safe, albeit in need of a long, hot bath!

Several years ago, I petitioned the president of Rwanda to build a more hospitable road from Kigali to Kibeho, given the sheer number of people who make the trip. Kibeho is a treasure to the world, similar to Lourdes in France and Fátima in Portugal. Miracles happen there on a daily basis, and increasing access to them will be beneficial to all of us. Thankfully, within the last year, a paved road from the city of Butare was built to take pilgrims to Kibeho—and it is only a 25-minute journey. I pray that when Mary's request for two chapels is finally fulfilled, the road(s) to Kibeho will be safe, smooth, and accessible to everyone.

## THE PILGRIMS OF KIBEHO

Kibeho is well loved by people around the world and receives anywhere from 30,000 to 50,000 visitors during peak season. I am fortunate to be able to visit Rwanda three times a year, when I take people, including devout Catholics and those who consider themselves to be spiritual but not religious, on pilgrimage. Usually, I am there for seven days at a time, three of which are spent entirely in Kibeho. The largest group of people I've taken to Kibeho was 65 total. Often, at least 20 percent of the group I take at any given time comprises individuals who've accompanied me on previous pilgrimages to Kibeho. And the more they make the pilgrimage to this sacred site, the more they fall in love with it.

I offered my first unofficial pilgrimage to Kibeho in 2007. I was speaking at a Hay House event when a woman stood up and excitedly proclaimed, "We should go with Immaculée to Rwanda!" A group of people, most of whom were not Catholic, immediately expressed interest.

In Kibeho, I explained to them that if they approached Mary as a loving mother to whom they could talk about anything in their lives, she would hear their prayers and work to grant them. On our first trip to the Shrine of Our Lady of Sorrows, I encouraged them to sit in contemplation and prayer while I stepped away for 15 minutes to have my own sacred time with Mary. When I returned to the group, I was surprised to see that all of them were in tears!

"What happened?" I asked, worried that something unfortunate had befallen this group of faithful foreigners.

One woman who was able to speak through her tears responded, "It's so beautiful here. It's a feeling like nothing we've ever felt—like there's someone who genuinely cares about us." Others in the group went on to say that it almost felt as if some loving being had placed their hands over each person, offering a sense of refuge and comfort.

I knew that Our Lady had touched these pilgrims, just as she touches anyone who comes to her with an open heart. This experience gave me the confidence to dedicate myself to regularly taking people on pilgrimage to Kibeho. I would share my own story with others in order to make myself a messenger of Mary. Whatever happened after that would occur by God's grace.

In 2009, I took travelers with me on my first official pilgrimage to Kibeho. I even publicized it on my website, which was a completely new tool for me. I'd been told that if I wanted to share the miracles of Kibeho with others, I needed to move beyond the word-of-mouth approach. Altogether, 14 people, all of whom were strangers to me, signed up for the pilgrimage. One thing I hadn't bargained for was the wave of panic that came over me just before the trip. For some reason, I became overwhelmingly fearful. While I trusted my message and Mary wholeheartedly, I found myself contemplating several worst-case scenarios: What if someone got into an accident or became ill? What if the people in the group, none of whom I'd previously met, didn't like Rwanda, or felt disconnected from the purpose of the pilgrimage? I immediately called my agent and said, "Please tell everyone who signed up for this trip that I'm not going because I'm sick. We'll give them their money back." My agent begged me to change my mind, but I was resolved. Then, one of my closest friends, a fellow Rwandan who now lives in Belgium, bolstered my confidence. She said, "Immaculée, I'll go with you on this trip and be with you every step of the way. If you ever feel scared or anxious, you can tell me what's going on, and I can step in and take your place if you need me to. I know they will be happy. You always tell me stories about Kibeho, and as your friend, I am so touched. Please tell them your stories. And take them there. Mary will touch them too. Don't be scared."

Tears filled my eyes at her generous offer. I truly felt as if angels from heaven had come to allay my fears and reassure me that God and Mary would be present with me if I simply got out of my own way and allowed the pilgrimage to happen.

Of course, the group had a transformative journey. We prayed the Seven Sorrows and the traditional rosary every day during that trip. Just like the unofficial pilgrimage, this one was filled with tears of joy and catharsis as everyone bonded over their shared experiences. At the end of our journey, many of them looked at me in disbelief: "Is this it? Are we done? Are we really never going to meet again?"

"Not necessarily," I said. "What if we prayed the Seven Sorrows Rosary every day for nine days in a novena?" And so we did! But after the nine days were over, the group had the same inquiry: Was this really the end of our journey of faith and devotion together?

I suggested that we take another 30 days to pray the rosary. At this time, Zoom wasn't an option, so we decided that we would connect via e-mail to discuss our experiences. Of course, after the month was up, people were still finding ways to stay connected! We ended up praying together for six months, and this period of time cemented our bonds as eternal sisters and brothers.

Many fruits came out of this experience. In fact, one woman from the first official pilgrimage became a helper of sorts, as she volunteered to come with me wherever I spoke—whether I was offering retreats about Our Lady of Kibeho or teaching the Seven Sorrows Rosary—so that she could witness and assist me. Thirteen years later, she still travels with me! Another woman who'd accompanied me on that pilgrimage insisted, "You can't keep this wonderful information to yourself and those lucky few who get to go with you to Kibeho! I'll prepare a retreat in the U.S. so you can bring Mary to everyone." She lived in Louisiana, and she subsequently helped to organize three retreats at which I shared Mary's healing message.

Over the years, I have seen how Mary's message has changed people's lives and made them more receptive to their purpose on this earth. Many pilgrims end up forming their own charitable or religious organizations; others decide they will devote their lives to volunteer work and helping those who are greatly in need of hope and salvation.

The miracles I've encountered have ranged from the mundane to the unbelievable. One man who has accompanied me on pilgrimages was accustomed to debilitating chronic illness, which would leave him bedridden for two to three months at a time. He told me that in using the Seven Sorrows Rosary, he was able to push through both the physical and emotional pain. Since he began praying the rosary, his life took a whole new direction. Today, he is full of vitality and joy, and he has never fallen back into his illness.

I especially love witnessing the transformation that takes hold of Americans who are visiting Rwanda for the first time. For the first few days, people are on their phones and immersed in their lives back home, full of their creature comforts and preoccupations. However, there is a joy and simplicity in my home country that is contagious. Although people are poor, they know what it means to love and to connect from the heart. This seems to disarm foreign visitors. By the third or fourth day in Rwanda, visitors have practically abandoned their phones (except for the purpose of taking photos of this majestic country). Whereas they might have also been overly concerned with their clothing and appearance early in the trip, their prior self-absorption gives way to a sweetness, a togetherness that I believe many of us the world over yearn for.

I believe that Rwanda, and especially Kibeho, are places that allow us to open up to our capacity for joy and love because they have been touched by Mary's grace. People come to recognize that they need not stew in their problems alone and disconsolate. They can give their tears and fears to Our Lady; they can cry with her, and their pain will heal.

The miracles I've encountered (many of which I share throughout this chapter) include healing from infertility, cancer, and addiction; emerging from the heavy weight of grief; and experiencing a greater sense of purpose and connection. I know without a doubt that when we honor Our Lady, she is there to console us and to reveal the many opportunities for healing and growth that God has generously offered anyone who follows his way.

Mary's presence is palpable to anyone who moves toward her with love and a genuine desire to receive her messages, but it is especially palpable in Kibeho, from the moment you set foot onto the hallowed ground of the shrine and gaze up at her beautiful statue. In addition to the statue, which exudes grace and beauty, the area near the shrine includes a Garden of the Blessed Virgin Mary that is made up of many flowers, plants, trees, and benches where pilgrims can sit in contemplation. Aside from offering a restful outdoor sanctuary for travelers, the garden also brings us back to the ways that flowers and trees often showed up as powerful symbols in the Marian apparitions. The visionaries of Kibeho had the privilege of entering a liminal heavenly realm in which they often saw fields full of flowers. At the Blessed Virgin's request, the girls were asked to water trees and flowers, which symbolized the many people receiving and taking Mary's message to heart. As Mary explained to the visionaries, the number of conversions would increase the "field of flowers." In fact, Mary would often say that all people are her own flowers—all of us representing our own unique beauty and potential, despite differences in race, ethnicity, tribe, or nation.

Everyone is welcome in Kibeho and should feel at home here, for Mary always intended for this place to be for all her children. She told the visionaries that heaven has touched this place, and the blessings remain for all those who seek them. My hope is that flowers from around the world will continue to gather in Kibeho, and that the beautiful garden that came to be there will only continue to flourish and spread. Remember, we are all Mary's flowers.

## THE PENITENT HUSBAND

I have saved literally hundreds of e-mails from people around the world detailing their own encounters with the Seven Sorrows Rosary and the ways it has transformed their lives. I have personally heard of a number of wonderful blessings bestowed on those who have prayed this magnificent rosary: women becoming pregnant after many heartbreaking years spent trying to conceive; people being healed from so-called terminal cancers after having been told by doctors they would be dead within months or weeks; chronically unemployed people suddenly finding fulfilling, permanent jobs; and still others who were released from decades of debilitating drug and alcohol addiction and the despair of crippling depression.

One of the most moving stories of transformation I can think of is the story of a husband and wife that occurred in Kibeho several years ago, and that I heard about from a close friend and fellow devotee of Mary.

There was a kind and purehearted woman who belonged to a group of people who referred to themselves as the Flowers of Kibeho. Together, they would pray for one another, as well as their families and the people of Rwanda. They would often go to the Shrine of Our Lady of Sorrows to offer their prayers and to share their own personal trials with Our Lady. This particular woman happened to have a husband who would get very drunk; when he stumbled home at night, he would fly into an incoherent rage and kick the poor woman out of her own home before falling asleep. The couple's children would open the door and bring their mother back into the house, but only when their father was fully asleep.

The woman, who was very religious, loved her husband and didn't want to leave him. She joined a prayer group known as the Flowers of Mary to pray for his deliverance from his addiction and his abusive behavior. At the same time, she decided, "This man was given to me by God, so whatever he asks of me, I will respect it. I will take it as I would from God. Whatever pain he gives me, I'm going to learn to bear it. I will let this be a way to atone for my sins. I will do my part to love my husband and see what God does with both him and me. I will also ask Mary to pray for me."

Certainly, not all women would be willing to put themselves in such a thankless situation, but she had complete faith in Mary and knew in some way that her suffering would ultimately be worth it.

The next time her husband came home drunk and ordered her to leave the house, she did so without protest. When her children came to let her back in, she said, "Your father told me to leave the house, so I did. I am simply obeying my husband's words, and I will not hear you speak ill of him."

When her husband awakened and realized that his wife was not there, he went outside and found her. "Why are you outside?" he asked, seemingly astonished and unable to remember his terrible behavior from the previous night.

"You asked me to leave the house," she explained. "I decided to listen to you because you're my husband."

He was baffled by his wife's response, which was full of calmness and docility. Instead of being abrasive or angry, she was being respectful and seeking his permission! What was happening?

Soon it was time for the group to go to Kibeho, so the wife asked her husband for permission to go with them. He assented, but unbeknownst to her, he followed them in his car, perhaps to understand why this was such an important trip for his wife. Moreover, her unfazed attitude had taken him aback, and he suspected that her work with the Flowers might be behind this. He wanted to see what was behind his wife's strange behavior.

As the group prayed in the church, he hid in the back corner. He watched them attending mass and praying the rosary. Then the group exited the church and prostrated before the statue of Mary. The husband watched them silently, not understanding why they were engaged in this grand display of devotion. He was not a religious man by any means, and he felt little connection to Mary or Jesus.

By this time, the wife realized that her husband had followed the group all the way to Kibeho. By 5:30 P.M., it was already getting dark, and it was time to leave, but her husband's car was still there, meaning he was still on the premises. She asked one of her friends, "Can we wait for my husband? The road is so dark at night, and it would be good if we could let him drive behind us."

The group agreed, and they continued to wait for her husband. Finally, the woman asked her friend to see what her husband was doing and to let him know that it was time to leave, otherwise the road would be much too treacherous to navigate. The friend came back to inform her that her husband had been kneeling before the statue of Mary, weeping, and that he'd requested for his wife to come to him. As she approached her husband, curious as to what had happened, she saw that his expression and disposition had completely changed. His eyes were filled with grief as he asked her, "Is it possible for you to forgive me for everything I have put you through?"

Of course, she instantly said yes and attempted to embrace him, but he said, "Don't touch me now. I can explain when we get home."

Later, when they were both home, the husband revealed the miracle that had occurred when he'd stood before Mary's statue. "The most beautiful woman I have ever seen came directly out of the statue! She was filled with brightness and goodness. She just looked at me, and then she showed me visions of you . . . of the sadness and pain you feel when I'm mean to you. I could also see our children under the covers, crying about how I treat you. She showed you praying for me all the while, and I felt terrible. I already felt bad about what I'd done, but then the woman showed me many vivid pictures of hell and informed me that I would be going there if I continued on this path! She informed me that I was only able to see and understand her because of all your prayers for me! She told me that God would forgive me, but that I'd have to ask for your forgiveness and tell you all the things I've done that you don't know about."

His wife sat there patiently and listened to her husband confess all his wrongdoings, which included infidelity and dabbling in black magic. He was deeply ashamed, but his wife could tell that he had already fully repented.

Today, he is a changed man. Aside from recommitting himself to his wife and family, he joined the Flowers of Kibeho and now teaches the Seven Sorrows Rosary to others—reminding them of the power of baring our hearts and unburdening ourselves of the suffering that we carry . . . and that we sometimes unconsciously pass on to others. He came to realize that there is no king without a queen—and just as God is in his heaven, Mary is always here on earth to intercede on our behalf and bring us back into God's fold whenever we've gone astray.

## THE PROMISE OF A CHILD

Although it is good to pray to saints and ask for their intercession (including St. Monica, the patron saint of mothers and the mother of St. Augustine, whose conversion she'd prayed for, for nearly 30 years), it is the Blessed Virgin to whom most Christian mothers pray. Historically, Mary has always reminded the world that she is especially responsive to the prayers of mothers. Of all the people on our planet, it is mothers who continue to display unwavering, unconditional love for their children, in good and bad times. Mary herself was exactly the same—and her heart is with all mothers and mothers-to-be who experience suffering of any kind, regardless of their religious affiliation.

A few years ago, I experienced the intercession of Mary in the area of childbirth and infertility firsthand. A man I knew had a daughter who was a model in New York, so he asked me if I'd meet up with her. We met for coffee, and she confided that she was having difficulty conceiving. She had gone through in-vitro fertility treatments and other painful procedures, but with no success. It was clear that she was disappointed, depressed, and desperate for a better way.

I don't typically discuss religion with people unless it is a topic of conversation that's already on the table, but I knew from my own experience of the miracles associated with Mary and childbirth that I had to share my knowledge with this woman. "I'm not sure if I should tell you this or not," I admitted, "but there is a prayer that has helped many women to become pregnant, sometimes after years of difficulty with conceiving. It's called the Seven Sorrows Rosary, and it's one of the Virgin Mary's gifts to this world." I explained to her that the rosary is especially powerful when it comes to healing the tears of mothers, as Mary, too, was a mother who suffered for her child. "I can teach you how to pray this rosary," I suggested. The woman was not religious, but she was willing to try.

As I was teaching her the prayer, I tried to emphasize that it is not meant to be a magical panacea that will automatically grant people's wishes. Mary sees into our hearts, and when we pray with the willingness to recognize the suffering she lived through, it's almost as if we are making space in our hearts for greater compassion, love, and faith. This is a catalyst for miracles.

As the woman and I sat and meditated on what happened to Mary, she began to cry. "It's hard to see how one person could go through that," she said. I smiled and replied, "Yes, and now she is the Queen of Heaven and Earth who has positioned herself as a helper to humanity, because she knows what we go through when we suffer."

We prayed together for a while, and then the woman moved to China for a job. Incredibly, within two weeks of moving, she sent me an exuberant e-mail sharing that she was pregnant with twins! I have no doubt that her kindness and receptivity in opening her heart to Mary and Jesus's suffering were crucial aspects of her prayer being answered. For when you join your heart to Mary's, just as she shared with the visionaries of Kibeho, there is nothing she will not do for you.

I have heard at least a hundred cases of people who shared that they became pregnant after praying the Seven Sorrows Rosary. Mary is especially receptive to those women who long for a child, and I receive letters and accounts on a regular basis about the answered prayers of those who have struggled with infertility for years.

In 2012, I received the following e-mail from a lovely woman who wished to share the miraculous news of her daughter-in-law giving birth to a daughter:

*Dear Immaculée,*

*I want to tell you about a miracle that happened as a result of Mary's intercession because of prayers offered while using the Rosary of the Seven Sorrows. My son and daughter-in-law had lost three babies and were told by reproductive specialists in the state of New Mexico that they would probably never be able to have healthy children. They had been married for seven years.*

*In 2010, my sister and I came to your talk in New Mexico. You mentioned the miracles of the Seven Sorrows Rosary and told us of several cases of women who became pregnant through its intercession. After your talk, I bought several rosaries and went to see my son and daughter-in-law. I told them exactly what you had told us. I told them that I was going to pray for the miracle of a baby, but I would also pray that if God chose not to give them a baby, they would still share full and loving lives together. Then we all started to pray.*

*In the fall of 2011, I came back to your retreat, and you told us once again about the power of the Seven Sorrows Rosary. Much to our delight, our prayers were answered—my daughter-in-law conceived, and little Maggie was born on May 17, 2012! She is a healthy, beautiful baby with an angelic smile! She will be baptized tomorrow, August 5, in the same church in which you held your retreat. What joy there is in our family! Another miracle is that Maggie's parents were not practicing their faith, but now they have been going to mass and are taking Maggie with them!*

*Thank you for introducing the Seven Sorrows Rosary to us. We will continue to pray it regularly. May God bless you for continuing to share God's and Mary's message with the world. Know that we are praying for you and for your mission.*

*Much love,*
*M. B.*

It always warms my heart when I read stories like these about people whose faith is resuscitated when they pray the Seven Sorrows Rosary. Usually, people can trace the pregnancy directly back to their engagement with the prayer. Another couple who had been trying to conceive for seven years (there's that number seven again!) prayed the rosary, utilizing my advice to pray with their entire hearts and spirits, such that they would feel for Mary and Jesus; far beyond viewing them as historical figures in the distant past, they would think about them as if they were real people enduring hardship and suffering. Seven months later, the couple contacted me to share that they were having a baby! In fact, the first day they said the Seven Sorrows Rosary was the day they discovered she was pregnant.

One of my favorite stories about Mary interceding to help a woman who longed to be a mother took place in Rwanda. I recently heard about a village in Rwanda in which there was a procession with a statue of Mary; people prayed and sang as they walked with the statue throughout the village. For Catholics and those who love Mary, we believe that wherever her statues are, she is there too. And when we make a procession for Mary, blessings come to everyone in the village.

Along the way, a woman who was due to have her baby in just 10 days came to see the procession. She was not a Catholic; rather, she was an Adventist. Although she would be going into labor very soon, she was concerned about whether this would be a viable pregnancy. This was her fifth pregnancy, and all her previous children had been born after arduous C-section operations. Her doctor had warned her that this pregnancy could prove to be fatal, and there was a possibility she might not live through it. She was so worried that she'd been mostly in bed for the past few months, awaiting her due date and an operation that could result in her death.

As the procession passed by, she asked her husband to help her outside, where she gazed upon the statue and uttered the following prayer silently, from her heart: "Dear Mother of Jesus, Mary, if you are truly present with your statue, don't leave me this way. You are a mother, so you know what this is like. I am tired, and I am scared, so please help me to deliver safely. Keep my baby safe. Pray for me so that I may live to take care of my other babies too. Pray for us."

That same night, she started to feel labor pain, even though it was 10 days early. Before she had a chance to go to the hospital, she delivered a healthy baby—naturally, without surgery and without a doctor present, for the first time! It happened so quickly that the family had to call a nearby midwife for help. Today, this family often attends church, and their lives have transformed as a result. Although they are not Catholic, they go to Kibeho often to pray to Mary and to offer their gratitude.

Mary once told the visionaries of Kibeho, "To those who pray the Seven Sorrows Rosary, I will give peace to their families." In that sense, Mary's love extends to vulnerable young children, which is evinced in the following e-mail I received from one of my retreat participants:

*Immaculée,*

*I wanted to share with you that the Seven Sorrows Rosary has been a blessing to my family. It has helped me survive the past three years of my life. Thank you for sharing it with the world.*

*In September 2017, my daughter, Gianna Grace, named after Saint Gianna and the Blessed Mother, was born. Hearing loss led to an MRI, and at just four weeks old, she was diagnosed with a massive, inoperable tumor that was wrapped around her brain stem. She was sent home from the hospital on palliative care and was given weeks to months to live. Many, many people mailed our family relics, rosaries, medals, and holy water. Strangers and priests from all over came to hold and pray over her. We took her to shrines and churches. I read your e-mails every morning, as well as other daily scriptures. My husband and I finally surrendered to God's will for her.*

*My son's preschool teacher gave me a brown wooden Seven Sorrows Rosary with the meditations. I started meditating on the Blessed Mother's and Jesus's sufferings. I prayed continuously. I could relate to so many of the sorrows. I fell asleep each night wearing and clenching the rosaries, and prayed with all my heart. As I awoke every morning realizing that this nightmare was real, the prayer helped calm me enough so I could get through the day.*

*One of my best friends who lived across the state in Pittsburgh asked if she could set up a conference line so she could pray with me. Our Seven Sorrows prayer group spread. Every Tuesday, more and more family and friends would call a conference number at 9 P.M. to pray the Seven Sorrows Rosary. Between 50 and 100 people now join us in prayer each week on this call. We never miss it, not even during months of living in the hospital.*

*Our one-year-old daughter has had 6 brain surgeries; 12 general surgeries on her eyes, ears, and chest; MRI and CT scans every two to three months; 15 months of intensive chemotherapy; and countless blood draws, transfusions, and X-rays. She was sent home from a long hospital stay on a feeding tube. We've had doctors telling us that they're not sure how she's living after seeing her scans, and they're not sure how she'll be neurologically if she lives. She couldn't hear (there were weeks during her surgeries when I believe she couldn't see), she couldn't smile, there was a month where she couldn't open her mouth, her eye deviated inward, she had difficulty breathing and swallowing, and she had difficulty moving her left side. We continued to pray unceasingly. We prayed the Seven Sorrows Rosary and the Surrender Novena.*

*At six months old, Gianna started chemo to try to help shrink the tumor that was caused by a very rare blood disease called histiocytosis. The tumor was slowly responding to the treatment. She pulled out her feeding tube and continued breastfeeding. She now eats everything. She was taken off hospice care at eight months old. She started responding to sound at one year old and is now hearing and talking. She started half smiling. She has difficulties with her eyes, but she can see. She has difficulty with her balance, but she can walk and is trying to run and jump. She continues to heal and get stronger every day. There is finally some light at the end of our very dark tunnel.*

*My family has spent more time in the children's hospital than we have at home with her. I have met and fallen in love with so many kids and families on the oncology floor. I purchase rosaries from your store and have been sharing them with these families in need of faith and hope. I hope it helps them as it has helped us. I cried to my priest that we see so many very sick children at the hospital every day. I told him that it's not fair for me to ask for a miracle for Gianna because all of these beautiful children need one. He told me, "God does perform miracles. Why not your daughter?"*

*My husband and I only choose to share Gianna's story and the power of the rosary to share God's grace and the importance of prayer. We hope other families in our situation never give up hope. Something we learned through the past year is, "Having faith in God includes faith in his timing."*

*We continue to pray the Seven Sorrows Rosary every Tuesday with our prayer group for Gianna's continued healing and for other children and adults.*

*Love and prayers,*
*K. M.*

*P.S. There is a little more to Gianna's story. When Gianna was first put on hospice care, I had a dream that she was walking up the stairs at the art museum in Philadelphia. At the top of the stairs was Gianna Emmanuelle, the daughter of the saint Gianna was named for, and Pope Francis. A week after Gianna turned one year old, my dream came true. Pope Francis took Gianna off the side of the road and kissed and blessed her. Ironically, her tumor significantly decreased after her next scan. We believe that Pope Francis is a living saint, and we believe that God performs miracles. We believe Gianna's entire life is a miracle—from her birth, to the papal kiss, to her continuing to beat the odds in her healing. Please keep Gianna and her friends battling brain tumors in your prayers. Thank you.*

As this woman's priest had the good sense to remind her, God does perform miracles—and the Blessed Mother is here to intercede on our behalf. I encourage you to love Mary, who is the mother that Our Lord gave all of us when he was on the cross. If we love and respect her, and speak to her as if she were our own mother, she will always come to our aid. Trust me when I say that there are no coincidences. When we do our part and show up with love and reverence, and when we come to pray with heartfelt requests, God will always be there for us.

## AN ANTIDOTE TO ADDICTION

Another request that I've encountered quite often over the years is the prayer to release loved ones from the demons of addiction, which have the power to tear a family apart. I've known so many people who've watched helplessly as their children, partners, friends, and other family members entered the frightening downward spiral of drugs. Thankfully, the Seven Sorrows Rosary is one of the guiding lights that can carry a person through the pain of addiction and deliver them into the light of God's love.

I recall meeting a woman from Kansas City who informed me that her daughter was addicted to heroin and was currently living on the streets. Her daughter was an intelligent young woman who had dropped out of college because of the ravages of heroin, which had turned her life upside down. Her mother was desperate to help her daughter, but like so many people who have witnessed the demise of drug-addicted loved ones, she had exhausted her resources to help. She told me, "I'll try anything at this point. If the Seven Sorrows Rosary helps her, I'll bring her to your events so that I can speak about Mary's miracles." The mother bought two rosaries and two booklets describing how to say the Seven Sorrows Rosary—one for herself, and one for her daughter. She took a rosary to her daughter, who was homeless and on the streets, and she brought the other one home so that she could continue praying on her own.

One of Mary's promises was that if you pray the Seven Sorrows Rosary for anyone who is lost and not in a good state of mind, your prayer will be heard, and graces will fall upon them as if they themselves had sent the prayer out to God. To my amazement (but not my surprise), the woman I'd been in touch with brought her daughter to a retreat two years later. She was healthy, happy, and completely sober; her eyes shone with a brightness that seemed to counter the vicious cycle of addiction she'd been in not long before.

As they explained, the turning point in their story occurred when the daughter lost consciousness while she was living on the streets. She woke up one day in the hospital to discover that she'd been severely hurt and all of her belongings had been stolen. The only possession that remained with her was the Seven Sorrows Rosary her mother had given her, which had been in her hands when she was found unconscious. She had no recollection as to who had put it there. When the hospital called her mother, she knew instantly that it was a miracle from heaven and a sign from Mary that God had been watching over her child.

The tragedy of the moment gave way to a breakthrough. The daughter healed from her injuries and moved back home—and she never touched drugs from that day forth. Now she prays the Seven Sorrows Rosary every day to commemorate her near brush with death, as well as her deliverance from the clutches of a deadly addiction—all because of the care and protection of Our Mother.

## RECOVERY FROM ILLNESS

One of the most common themes in our understanding of miracles is the sudden recovery from chronic or terminal illness, even though in most cases the recipients of these miracles have been previously informed that their chances of survival are slim at best. Stories of miraculous healing were common in the time of Jesus's ministry, when he became well-known throughout Judaea for healing the sick.

Illness is a unique form of suffering that can take people to death's door and either close their hearts because of fear or open them because of faith. So it is little wonder that many of the miracles associated with the Seven Sorrows Rosary attest to the fact that a medical diagnosis is not the end of the road as far as God is concerned.

I have witnessed a slew of miracles among cancer patients who prayed the Seven Sorrows Rosary. One woman from Poland who came to one of my retreats had stage 4 breast cancer and was informed that there was nothing doctors could do. She and her husband took an entire weekend to pray the Seven Sorrows Rosary, from sunup to sundown. In this period, they poured their entire selves into the prayer, joining together until they were just one voice calling out to heaven. The woman had an appointment with her doctor the following Tuesday; when she showed up, they were dumbfounded to discover that the cancer had completely disappeared.

Another retreat participant told me that she'd had stage 4 pancreatic cancer, and at one point her doctor had given her six months to live. Before she met me, she connected with someone who had previously attended one of my retreats and who decided to assemble a Seven Sorrows Rosary prayer group to help the woman through her situation. The group prayed the rosary every day; two months later, when the woman visited her doctor, there was no trace of her cancer whatsoever.

It is my experience that the mind cannot understand what is best left to the domain of the heart. We can use reason and logic for many things in our world, but miracles defy explanation— because trust, love, and faith are not manufactured through the intellect but through God's will.

## HEALING FROM GRIEF, ANGER, AND NIGHTMARES

Healing our lives goes beyond healing our bodies. Many of us today are in need of emotional and spiritual healing. The power of the Seven Sorrows Rosary to bring people together and open our hearts to the deep forgiveness and healing that are God's gift to his children cannot be underestimated. Countless people have written to me about the transformations their lives have undergone on the deepest levels after surrendering their hearts to the Seven Sorrows Rosary.

A woman who came to one of my retreats had lost her mother to cancer at the age of 14. She told me, "It was not until the last night of praying with you that I realized the one I was angry with and needed to forgive was God. I still harbored anger and blame toward him. Thank you for freeing my soul."

Many of the people I've met have shared that the Seven Sorrows Rosary has helped them to resuscitate a relationship with God and work through their own resentments and bitterness. We forget that we merely persist in punishing ourselves when we armor our hearts against God—and Mary is here to help us to become softer so that we can truly receive his blessings rather than hold them at bay.

Another woman shared that her trust in God was renewed after learning the Seven Sorrows Rosary. "I truly, undoubtedly believe that God does listen and care. I often get discouraged, but now I understand the importance of love and faith. Without it, nothing can happen."

Many of my retreat participants are not Catholic or Christian, but they are drawn to the message of love, forgiveness, and miracles that I strive to convey in my work. Many of them have expressed doubt in God's love for them, but they come to realize that heartfelt prayer in which we are willing to pour out our fears and frustrations is the fastest way to know Mary and God—because we do away with pretenses and come to them with our full authenticity.

Many people tell me, "Thank you for reminding me that Jesus chose to come to us through Mary and that it is okay to go to him through Mary." While some might view God as a remote figure shrouded in immense mystery, Our Mother is immediately approachable. One of my retreat participants revealed that she was touched in a variety of ways, and that she learned about the power of "forgiveness, hope, repentance, miracles, and the love of Our Father and Blessed Mother. But the biggest, most powerful impact you've had on me was to introduce me to Our Mother Mary in a way I have never known her before. I am 41 and have been Catholic all my life, and this is the first time I feel a connection and a relationship with Our Lady Mother. Thank you, Immaculée. I feel the healing begin."

The miracles of the Seven Sorrows go beyond "asking for" specific things to happen. They also enable us to walk in Jesus and Mary's path with all our thoughts, words, and deeds. In transforming ourselves, we have a better opportunity to help others transform and find peace. When we connect with Mary, who lived a full and devoted life, we start to emulate her qualities. Countless times, I have heard from people who experienced major breakthroughs in their ability to be patient, forgiving, and open-hearted—similar to the Rwandan woman whose husband ended up turning his life around. Instead of asking for other people or external situations to change, we can pray for an internal transformation. One woman shared with me: "I have a new desire to forgive my 18-year-old grandson for his outlook on life right now. I pray to Mary to help me support him instead of putting him down, and I trust that God will change his attitude in due time."

The Seven Sorrows Rosary has the power to alleviate our internal chaos in all its manifestations. One woman sent me the following e-mail:

*Dear Immaculée,*

*Seven months ago, my mother died and I had been having horrible nightmares, so much so that I would try not to go to sleep. A few days later, my priest told me about the Seven Sorrows Rosary, which I'd only vaguely heard of before, and he suggested that I start saying it. He told me the Seven Promises of Mary, but particularly the fifth one: "I will defend them in their spiritual battles with the infernal enemy, and I will protect them at every instant of their lives."*

*I have to admit that I wasn't overly keen, but I was desperate to stop the nightmares. So, a couple of nights later, I fell asleep while saying the prayer, and although I still had nightmares, I didn't wake up with the feeling of fear I usually did. Somehow, I could "feel" Mary holding my hand, and I was at peace. I was still incredibly tired and fell asleep again a few hours later—NO NIGHTMARES!*

*Thank you, Blessed Mother, for accepting me as your child. Now that my own mother isn't here anymore, I need you even more. I understand just a tiny part of what you must have felt at each of your sorrows. My son is just a few years older than Jesus was when he was crucified.*

*If anyone reading this hasn't yet prayed the Seven Sorrows Rosary, please, please do.*

*V.*

All of these accounts reveal an important truth: there is nothing too big or small for us to bring to Our Mother and Our Father. They have the power to melt away the fog of confusion, anger, grief, and sorrow in which many of us are aimlessly wandering. I know that by God's grace, my own path for my life is clear, because I understand the mission he has put before me.

Each of us has a God-given purpose on this earth, and the Seven Sorrows Rosary can lead us directly to it so that we, too, can identify the unique ways we might work to alleviate the sorrow that has swept over our world.

Whether you wish to know true love, heal from illness, or be a more loving parent, always remember that Mary is here for you. Even when the days and nights are dark and cold, and you have strayed very far from your path, Our Mother is always home with the light turned on, waiting for you to return to her so that she can shower the blessings of God upon you.

## CHAPTER 13

# THE PRAYER GROUP

*Let your reasonableness be known to everyone. The Lord is at hand;*
*do not be anxious about anything, but in everything by prayer and*
*supplication with thanksgiving let your requests be made known to God.*
*And the peace of God, which surpasses all understanding,*
*will guard your hearts and your minds in Christ Jesus.*

— PHILIPPIANS 4:5–7

There is a special ritual in my life that I look forward to every day. After hours of busy activity—connecting with loved ones, planning retreats and pilgrimages, giving interviews, and working feverishly on my own creative and humanitarian projects—I know that there is a place for me to unwind and relax . . . to fully drop into the experience of receiving the grace of God.

A few moments before 7 P.M., I light the candles on my altar, grab my Bible, and take my rosary in hand. Then, I log into the Zoom room where dozens of people around the world meet without fail on a daily basis. There, I know that I can put down the cares of the world and experience the joy of connecting with others through our similarities and differences—but most of all, through our devotion to Our Lady and Our Lord.

We gather for an hour and a half to three hours (for those who wish to stay longer) as we move through the Seven Sorrows and the traditional rosary together. We share our prayers for loved ones who might be going through difficult moments. Although many of us meet daily, some people are able to come only once or twice a week. Many people I know meet on either Tuesdays or Fridays, or both. Mary told Marie-Claire she wanted people to meditate on the Seven Sorrows Rosary on these days: Tuesday, when she first appeared to Marie-Claire to remind the world about the Seven Sorrows; and Friday, the day Our Lord died.

Although this virtual congregation of multiple boxes on a screen is not what many of us have been accustomed to for most of our lives, there is a palpable sense of upliftment, almost as if we are in a church group, pouring out our hearts and sharing our fears, hopes, and dreams with one another. There is a sacred glow that lights up the space as I gaze at the many squares on my screen and recognize that Holy Providence brought us together. As I look at the faces of people who have been meeting every day for the last two years, I am filled with a sense of wonder and possibility. I am reminded that we are more similar than different. I can almost feel Mother Mary beaming down at us—through the technical glitches, through the profound effort it took to gather across multiple different time zones. I can almost hear her saying, "My children, I am with you."

I have been part of prayer groups for most of my life, especially since it was Mary's request in Kibeho that everyone belong to a prayer group. I have fond memories of holding the hands of friends and family members, praying for one another and our loved ones during times of celebration and times of crisis. During the time of the Marian apparitions in Rwanda, I would gather with the people in my village on a weekly basis, for we had been enjoined by Mary to come together and share our hearts and souls in prayer. Mary once told us that if we convened prayer groups in Rwanda, the horror that was coming would not come. As we would later realize, Mary was referring to the genocide. Unfortunately, while some of us paid attention, many turned away and went about their daily lives, not feeling the need to pray for something that was not yet a reality. Sadly, while there were not enough people gathered together in community to prevent the genocide, it is not too late for us to respond to the crisis of our time.

## HOW COVID-19 BECAME AN OPPORTUNITY FOR CONNECTION

I will never forget the time I learned that the world was going into lockdown.

Living in a bustling place like New York City and being someone whose entire livelihood revolves around travel, I knew that the pandemic would be a life-changing experience. As the streets of New York City became more and more deserted, and restaurants and brick-and-mortar shops in my neighborhood closed for the foreseeable future, I knew that it would not be wise to give in to panic. I quickly understood what I was meant to do in response to the dire situation we'd collectively found ourselves in.

Many years ago, when I began giving talks in the United States and throughout the world, I encouraged the people who came to my events to create their own prayer groups. Whether these prayers included wishes for the recovery of sick loved ones, or petitions to find a good job or loving partner, or requests for a more loving and reverential world, I wanted people to know the cathartic experience of finding beauty and solidarity in the midst of our difficult contemporary lives.

By the time COVID-19 struck the world, I had had a regular prayer group with friends, but I quickly recognized that the joy of gathering together in person would have to be put on hold. As more and more countries around the world went into lockdown, and as the streets of New York City, where I live, began to resemble a ghost town, I could feel my heart sinking. However, I knew that God's will would prevail . . . and that I could be a part of helping people get through this period and emerge with greater strength than ever before. In those early days, it felt as if we were all hanging by a thread, attempting to predict when life would go back to normal and vacillating between relief for this time to go inward and panic over the prospect of death and disaster. As interminable as those days felt, I accepted that this was just a moment in time, and that I would find the best way to adjust to it and stay connected to my spiritual life in the process.

With every perceived challenge we face, God always gives us an opportunity. For years, people around the world had begged me to travel to their neck of the woods. I always did my best to grant requests to hold a workshop or retreat in areas as close as Sioux Falls, South Dakota, and as far-flung as Bosnia and Herzegovina. However, I am only one person, and the requests were often too numerous for me to fulfill. As my late friend Dr. Wayne Dyer used to say, "I know that you go wherever you are called, but you'll find that travel takes its toll."

When the pandemic began, I received a flurry of e-mails from people who had attended my retreats, workshops, and pilgrimages, as well as those who had read my books. Many of them had similar stories, rife with anxiety and uncertainty. Some could not afford to quit their public-facing jobs, and they worried about being exposed to the virus; others were panicking over the health of immunocompromised relatives. Everyone I heard from expressed fear. Some worried that life would never go back to normal. Others opined that "normal" had never been satisfying to begin with, but they were concerned over how health care, education, and how government would cope with this dramatic obstacle we were now all being asked to consider. I realized that because so many people were hurting, one of the things I could offer was a little hope—especially through the power and grace of the Seven Sorrows Rosary, which I knew had the capacity to open people's hearts and provide them with a sense of connection and security that can defy even the most horrific of predicaments.

The pandemic became the perfect time for the seed that had already been planted to flourish. I had found a way to connect with the people who needed me, without having to make the long journey to be with them. Like most other people in early 2020,

I knew very little about Zoom. But that quickly changed. I recognized that some of the technological shifts that were happening alongside the pandemic, to support people who were working remotely and help everyone find ways to gather in the midst of this enormous disruption to our daily lives, were actually beneficial. Whereas I was limited by time and geography in the past, Zoom had created a way to convene large groups of people across wide distances.

Thus, the online prayer group was formed.

I didn't advertise it; I simply responded to those who'd asked about it. We quickly began a WhatsApp group, which more than 250 people across the globe joined. We quickly began meeting on Zoom every day. Souls from all walks of life—parishioners, schoolteachers, auto mechanics, doctors, lawyers, stay-at-home moms, and practically anyone you can imagine—began to pray the Seven Sorrows Rosary together.

Once, when I spoke with my friend Yosefa, who was one of the many visionaries blessed with apparitions of Mary in Kibeho during the 1980s, I asked her what her mission was. Mary had given all the visionaries a specific mission. Marie-Claire's had been spreading the Seven Sorrows Rosary. Yosefa informed me that it was her mission to teach the world the traditional rosary and to encourage people to form prayer groups in which they prayed the rosary together. I was very excited about sharing my online prayer group for the Seven Sorrows Rosary with Yosefa, and she was extremely encouraging in turn.

As many of the visionaries understood, prayer is most effective when it is revealed through our actions—when it begins to meld with our daily activities and influence our interactions with the rest of the world. During the first year of COVID, my virtual prayer group met primarily to contemplate Mary's Seven Sorrows together. It felt hauntingly appropriate, because it allowed us to share in the collective grief that was sweeping across the world, and to ask Mary and Our Lord to hear our prayers. We specifically petitioned them to ensure that nobody in our group would contract severe COVID or die from this mysterious illness. One of the other aspects of the prayer group that was so vital was forming a safe space in which we could release our pandemic-related fears and return to our lives with greater ease, confidence, and hope. Remarkably, among all the people who joined our prayer group, nobody ever contracted severe COVID. Some people did contract the virus, and others died of old age, but we were protected from the worst outcomes of the pandemic. I attribute this to our commitment to showing up together every day to offer our heartfelt gratitude to Our Lady and Our Lord for all they went through. Because of their intimate knowledge of suffering, we knew that we could rely on them to protect us as we voyaged into a strange and unfamiliar future together.

I have deepened my friendships with the people in my prayer group, many of whom I have known for several years. Reverend John F. McHale, who has accompanied me on seven pilgrimages to Kibeho, has been part of the group since the beginning, even taking on a chaplain role among us all. He has expressed that he is continually inspired by the participants' devotion to Our Lady: "People pray for various intentions, but the collective prayer of the group has helped throughout this time, and our intentions have been granted. It is very uplifting. When you're praying with the same people on a regular basis, you feel a lot of support. It's an important time to be praying, because we see the ways the world has abandoned God, and how that is resulting in war and other tragedies. This group is responding to Our Lady's plea to join with her and bring the power of God into all situations."

Jayne Misra, whom I met when I visited Iowa State University several years ago to give a talk on the Rwandan genocide, was immediately drawn to Our Lady and the Seven Sorrows. For her, the prayer group is nothing less than "a true family, sharing our joys, sorrows, laughter, and lives. We just fall more deeply in love and grow in gratitude to God. We have many personalities, but Our Lady draws us together as one big family."

As I always like to tell people, everyone is welcome at the group—not just those who are Catholic or who have a preexisting relationship with Mary and Jesus. Jayne's husband, Manjit, a practicing Hindu, has begun to pray the Seven Sorrows Rosary and the three full traditional rosaries every night. Jayne notes, "Our Mother and Our Lord have asked us to join a prayer group and I see the fruit. We are each on this journey, and a shared journey is one where everyone is supported, loved, and treasured. We have all grown so much in these two years. Essentially, the prayer group is a school of Mary!"

Many of our participants have echoed Jayne's sentiments, noting that the prayer group is more like a family than a disparate group of individuals. Joan Njau, who is originally from Kenya but now lives in Boston, notes that the support of our "prayer warriors" (those who decide to fight their personal and spiritual battles with the help of God), was invaluable when she lost her sister recently. What could have been a time of pure sorrow became much more bearable, as her fellow group members continued to support her in prayer.

For Joan, the strength that she gets from being part of the group has paid off in powerful ways. "The prayer group has impacted my life very positively and made my faith grow in leaps and bounds," she says. Over the course of four years, Joan's green card had been denied due to technicalities. Understandably, this was a continued source of stress that Joan could do very little about. Joan joined the prayer group in April 2020—and by November 2020, her green card finally came through.

"When I first made my intentions for joining the prayer group, I included my green card as one of my prayer items," she says. "By God's grace, I was called for another interview [by U.S. Citizenship and Immigration Services] in August 2020, which rarely happens. I knew that the prayer group was also praying for me, so I had faith. The interview finally happened in October, and I got my green card in November."

Joan had complete faith that the Seven Sorrows Rosary, which she'd already been familiar with through her African prayer group in Boston, was a miracle worker. Today, she prays the rosary every day: "It has helped me with everything: getting a good job, going to school, becoming healthier after being sick. Although I am now in a foreign land, through the Seven Sorrows Rosary, I have never once lacked anything. I wish more people knew about this beautiful prayer. In our everyday sorrows, each of us can relate to Mary's journey."

As a devoted member of the group in the last two years, she adds, "I would not be anywhere else between 7 and 10 P.M. every day. Even if I'm at work, I just put my headphones on, because the prayer group is the highlight of my day."

I am always overjoyed to hear about participants' experiences, because they validate my awareness that in opening our hearts to the Seven Sorrows our own preoccupations are transformed, and we get to experience the joy and miracles that are the result of many diverse people coming together for one unified purpose. In many ways, I know that the fervent prayers of my prayer group, to ensure that the basilica requested by Our Lady would finally be built in Kibeho, have helped to alleviate the long delay and forge a path toward fulfillment. Through faith and connection, our prayers have the ability to transform our daily pitfalls and challenges into opportunities to rejoice. God never meant for us to suffer alone, in silence; his intention was always for us to join together in devotion with our brothers and sisters, and to share the contents of our hearts with one another and with him so that we, as beautiful parts of his creation, can be made new again.

## FREEDOM FROM THE VISE GRIP OF FEAR

In our time together, the people in the prayer group cocreated a powerful opportunity to find an outlet for grieving our human condition. Through this period, we witnessed births, deaths, social upheaval, and moments of grace and radiance. During that first year, we prayed the Seven Sorrows Rosary as well as the traditional rosary. After that, we prayed upon the other Christian miseries with the Joyful Rosary (reflecting on Mary's five experiences of exalted joy and hope), the Luminous Rosary (reflecting on five different aspects of Jesus's mission on earth), and the Glorious

Rosary (reflecting on the Resurrection of Jesus and its attendant gifts, as well as the love shown to Our Mother at the end of her earthly life).

One of the things the prayer group helps me remember is that when we are divided, we are conquered. The haunting example of the Rwandan genocide reminds me of this. When we begin to look at one another through eyes clouded by hatred and suspicion (another sad by-product of the pandemic), we are no longer under the grace and auspices of God. We throw off his cloak of protection and love, and we fall into sin and temptation. However, prayer from the heart can bring us back into connection with God, ourselves, and each other. The literal meaning of the word *community* is "with unity." It is this unity that helps us move through times of crisis with greater faith and love.

Mary is the perfect example of what it means to create a community in which God is at the center of our lives. Countless times, around the world, she has appeared to people and helped to resuscitate hope and love where previously there may have been very little. She has encouraged people to take on the mantle of responsibility when it comes to providing those around them with comfort and security. Our Lady takes our prayers to the altar of heaven and promises to provide solutions to each of the problems that plague our hearts. When I began the prayer group, I knew without a shadow of a doubt that Mary's love was the antidote to the suffering the world experiences today. In some ways, all of us are frightened and overwhelmed children who only need to feel the maternal warmth and protection of Our Mother in order to muster the courage to confront the world as it is today.

Of course, there are many different ways to pray. Not everyone I've met in these past two years has prayed for sustenance during the time of COVID. Some of us have prayed for grace in unexpected ways.

For example, I knew a very prayerful, reverent man who confided that he believed sacrifices would be necessary during this time of hardship. Unlike many, he actually felt at peace with dying from COVID; it was as if he were prepared long before he got it. He told me more than once, "I feel like I am on my way to Golgotha, and I need to rest. I can't wait to rest, to see my Lord, even if the way is not pleasant."

We are all going to die, and to die in peace is the most important thing of all. This man did not feel like an unfortunate victim. In fact, because he had lived a long and fulfilling life, he was ready to go. I have met many others who similarly told me that they wanted to die, as they felt they had done everything they could and just wanted to join God. They were not desperate or wanting to commit suicide—but they were ready to die, and ready for whatever God's will was for their life, including taking them to heaven.

In this way, our prayers need not solely be for protection from the harsh realities of the world, which include death. Anyone who lives is destined to die, and when we pray, we must learn to be reasonable. Through our prayer, we can face the truth of who we are and what we truly need in order to fulfill our heavenly purpose on this earth with peace and acceptance. We can do so, not from a place of fear and avoidance, but from a place of enthusiastically inviting God's will for us . . . free from fear. When it is our time to go, it is our time to go—and we can leave this world with a sense of peace, knowing that we will return to God's embrace.

While the virtual prayer group I started was meant to allay everyone's fears and offer a sense of protection, I have encountered many people who have allowed fear to conquer their hearts and fill them with defeat and foreboding. What I've discovered is that when it goes unchecked and unprayed, fear can be one of the most debilitating experiences of all, as it often leads us down dark and lonely roads, where we feel thoroughly alone, and we begin to strike out at others. (Have you ever noticed that the most violent people are often the people who are filled with the greatest fear?)

This is why I always remind others that even if they seem to be up against an insurmountable obstacle, such as receiving a fatal diagnosis or mourning a loved one in the throes of addiction, there is no need to worry. God grants peace to all those who ask for it, and he always hears the prayers of those who are in need. While we cannot predict the future or know how things will turn out, we can relinquish a false sense of control and give our worries to God.

During the genocide, I absolutely knew that I did not want to die at the hands of violent killers. Intellectually, I understood that many innocent people would die, but I sensed that I still had so much to experience. So I prayed for God to protect me, and he did. At the same time, I understand that there are so many people who courageously sacrificed their lives during the genocide, often in order to protect loved ones and strangers alike. But every single one of us reaps what we sow. My family members led simple, loving lives, and they were especially sensitive to the needs of their community. It breaks my heart to know that they died in ways that were not befitting of their kindness and benevolence, but I also know that we must endure many hardships in order to enter the Kingdom of God. Whether or not we find peace in this life, which is ephemeral, those of us who walk in God's footsteps—with compassion, fortitude, and humility—will find everlasting peace in God's Kingdom. In this way, whatever our fate may be, we can walk with the absolute knowledge that there is nothing to fear if we go about our days with a pure and reverent heart, bringing harm to none.

Often, we use prayers to ask for something we want. It is absolutely fine to request God's assistance; after all, Jesus said, "Ask and you will receive, and your joy will be complete" (John 16:24).

However, our acceptance of God's will, as well as the prayer to release the fear that might be shadowing our fate, is a powerful medicine that can remove earthly pain and shroud us in protection.

Please know that while we cannot count on the righteousness of other humans, God is good and will grant you peace if you ask for it. The best way to reach God is to pray—particularly through honoring the suffering of Our Lord and Our Lady. Again, reflecting on their suffering should not be cause for despair. By honoring their suffering, we come to heal from *our* suffering. We come to recognize every grief that has passed through our life, and in so doing we empty our hearts of darkness and fill up with the pure love and light of God. However, we can't experience this kind of peace if we have not healed what needs to be healed, whether it be anger, jealousy, fear, or anything that keeps us in a state of disconnection or inner and outer conflict.

If you are interested in starting your own prayer group, I encourage you to find a group of people with whom you can meet on a regular basis. Your group can meet for a variety of purposes: some of your prayers may be for the resolution of personal issues, while others may be on behalf of your city, country, or this beautiful planet on which we live.

One of the things that Mary told the visionaries in Kibeho is that if they came together in groups, their prayers would be even more powerful than if they had prayed alone. Remember that Jesus said, "For where two or three are gathered in my name, there am I in the midst of them" (Matthew 18:19–20).

If there's one lesson that has touched me throughout my life, it's that we need each other. So I encourage you to start a prayer group, in which you read the Bible together, say the Seven Sorrows Rosary together, unburden your hearts, and allow yourself to step directly into your grief—for yourself, your loved ones, and the world at large. As Mary told the visionaries in Kibeho, "Allow your hearts to feel—because if you don't feel, you won't know what others are feeling."

By refusing to be fractured on the basis of differing opinions or fear-based prejudice, we become stronger; and when we pray together, we grow stronger together. Through this process, we come to heal the wounds that threaten to weaken us. Through this camaraderie, we experience the power of compassion, empathy, and transparent vulnerability. We accept that we were made for these times—and that now is a time for us to pray together. Through our prayers, we can make what was broken whole again.

# CONCLUSION

## Our Lady's Promises Live On

I am so grateful that you chose to accompany me on this potent journey through the Blessed Virgin's Rosary of the Seven Sorrows. I hope that in reading about Mary's life and all she lived through, you were able to connect to your own stories of suffering and recognize that you're not alone . . . and that the only way out is through.

At the beginning of every day and at the end of every night, I find myself in deep prayer: prayer that all of us will know peace and alleviation from suffering; prayer that all of us will come to realize the gifts of Our Lord's sacrifice and Our Lady's intercession on behalf of each of us; prayer that we will overcome sin and remember that we were made in God's image—that our true nature is one of goodness and beauty.

I believe that it's possible for everyone to enter the kingdom of heaven, but only if we see and know the truth of our interconnectedness and God's will for us to act in accordance with his laws, which transcend any human-made laws because they come from the source of all love and wisdom.

The Seven Sorrows help us to recognize the many intricate threads that connect us together in the mystery of existence. Of course, this includes the reality of suffering, which all religions have acknowledged. The Seven Sorrows give us a real-life example of the intensity of suffering that plagues our planet. It does not ask us to pretend that everything is okay or to avert our gaze from this sobering reality.

"Whatsoever you do to the least of your brothers and sisters you do unto me," Our Lord famously said (Matthew 25:40). In remembering this, I am moved to sit, reflect, and ask myself whether I have seen God in those who pass through my life—from the people on the subway, to the clerks at the supermarket, to my friends and family, to the souls I meet on pilgrimages and retreats, and even those who have contributed to my misery in some way. Did I meet insult with injury, or with kindness and a prayer that the people who harmed me find their way back to God? Did I choose to open rather than close my heart, or did I only pay lip service to the truths uttered by Our Lord and Our Lady? Did I offer words of kindness and nourishment to people in grief? Did I offer food and drink to those who are hungry and thirsty? Did I uplift the destitute and lonely, or did I turn away because it was too difficult to make contact with their pain?

By connecting us to the suffering that Mother Mary lived through, the Seven Sorrows Rosary also connects us to the ubiquitous reality of suffering in our world. This always includes our own suffering. Certainly, it can be tempting to armor ourselves and refuse to take any of it in, especially with the constant onslaught of the 24-hour news cycle, or the tendency to doomscroll social media and find ourselves embroiled in arguments with strangers. Anguish and loss surround us on all sides, so I understand the urge to simply go about our lives as if none of what is happening around us has anything to do with us. But Mary's Seven Sorrows show us that our awareness of suffering is exactly what opens the doors to compassion and grace!

Through their suffering, Jesus and Mary saved our lives, our very souls. The punishment that was meted out to humans—for our ignorance, our persistent violence, and delusional behavior—was something that these two sinless souls experienced in full force . . . all out of pure love for us. Sometimes I wonder what would have happened if Mary had rejected Angel Gabriel's invitation to her. What if she had refused to be the Mother of Our Lord? Perhaps our salvation would have been delayed, or not even possible. But Mary did what Mary had always done, without conditions: she respectfully submitted to God's will, whatever the cost would be. In this way, she became our Mother and a model for what it means to live a godly life in which we fully recognize our responsibility to help create a paradise on this earth—to usher in God's Kingdom together.

As I've mentioned, when I first heard about the Seven Sorrows Rosary, the prospect of contemplating Mary's suffering was frightening. It was painful and depressing to think about.

I wanted to feel a sense of upliftment in my prayer, not agony! However, as soon as I got to know the rosary, I realized that this was not the kind of suffering that would depress or deplete me. It became the kind of suffering that uplifted me, because it revealed to me that there is hope at the heart of our human condition. The hope is the experience of compassion, which would not be possible without suffering. In fact, it is suffering that opens us up to the greatest truth of all: there is a God who loves us. And no matter what trials and tribulations we may experience in our earthly existence, God's love is always there to act as a beacon in times of desperation. The experience of finding light at the end of the tunnel, when you think you just can't go on, is one of the greatest experiences I can think of. So often, we tend to take our happiness for granted, but suffering transforms us. If we have walked through suffering, every small joy becomes a garden in full bloom lit up by a radiant sun. We come to truly feel the blessings of this life and recognize the beauty that is all around us—even when we cannot see it. This is God's message, his gift, to us.

I know from both my experience and the experiences of thousands of people that praying the Seven Sorrows Rosary, or even just meditating on the experiences of our Mother Mary, will make you feel loved. Anytime I miss my family, I find myself thinking of the nights my mother didn't sleep when I was sick; or the times my father canceled his meetings because I wasn't feeling well; or when my brother couldn't play with his friends because he was too busy consoling me. These moments buoy my spirits. They remind me of the compassion that has sustained me. They remind me that I have loved and that I have been loved. In some ways, even though I still feel grief over the loss of my family, my awareness of their love for me, which never waned as long as they lived, makes me feel a happiness and levity in my heart that I cannot explain.

The same is true when I contemplate the lives of Jesus and Mary. Their suffering is not like any other suffering. It is a medicine, a healing salve. When we choose to empathize with them, to open our hearts and love them as much as they love us, we reap the full benefits of their medicine.

I want to assure you that through the prayer of the Seven Sorrows Rosary you will experience healing. You will find answers to your questions and solutions to your problems. Perhaps you will even experience miracles. Whatever the case, know that the gifts will transcend your wildest expectations. By accepting your suffering and learning from it instead of cursing, complaining, blaming, or making excuses—you, too, will become part of the light that I believe is sweeping across this planet . . . the light that is helping us to see our own ignorance, to make amends for our sins, and to recognize that we are all part of God's family.

If you are reading this book, I know that you are no stranger to suffering. Perhaps you've had experiences that made your suffering difficult to endure. Perhaps you have lived through persecution, despair, disenfranchisement, alienation, and all of the struggles that are playing out on the world stage on a daily basis. Perhaps you have experienced suicidal ideation and felt that your pain was too much to endure. I have met many people who ended up taking their own lives because they believed this was the only solution. Every single one of us has felt this desperation to a certain degree, but as we pray the Seven Sorrows we see that there is another way.

Mary, too, felt that her life had ended after Jesus's death, but rather than trying to find a way out of the hell she was living, she continued to give everything to God—to live for, and be an instrument of, God's will. For some of us, that might sound daunting, or even as if we are giving our power away. But the truth is, when we allow ourselves to be carriers of God's will, when we have lost everything and feel there is no more to gain, God empties us out and makes us new again. God is the source of all our power, and it is only by living in God's will that we can truly experience happiness and purpose.

During my own times of suffering and those moments when I wanted to give up and collapse into nothingness, I begged Jesus and Mary to be near me and give me an iota of their strength. I continued to pray the rosary, to recite the words, even when I did not feel them. I prayed like a child repeating after her mother's words out of respect and faith. I didn't trust my own words, which were laced with enmity and uncertainty—so I prayed and prayed and prayed. I didn't know if any of it would end up working, but it didn't matter. My prayers saved me. Over time, they became food for my soul and gave me a newfound sense of self, as well as the courage and confidence I had always been searching for. Finally, I felt enveloped in peace. Even in the midst of my pain, I felt sheltered by goodness.

So, whatever you are going through, please know that the Seven Sorrows are a gift from heaven that Our Lady obtained for us. She promised her assistance and many graces to those who call upon God through this prayer. If you are facing any troubles or if your heart needs healing, take some time to integrate this prayer into your life. You will see through the veil of tears, through the cruelty that we tend to visit upon each other so relentlessly, and you will be transformed.

Remember that you always have a model in Mary. Mary never pretended. She allowed her heart to ache and her vulnerability to shine through. This genuine receptivity to her experience made her strong as steel—not because she armored herself from her feelings but because she let them be the path that always led her back to God.

Our Lady is here to help us, but she also asks that we help her in return. So I kindly ask you to share with me any miracles you experience with the Seven Sorrows Rosary, as your stories will help me to encourage others to pray it. Share the rosary with and teach it to those you love, or anyone who could use a boost from heaven. I promise you that the impossible will become possible, and Our Lady will surely reward you. She always does.

*May God Bless You!*
*Immaculée*

# ABOUT THE AUTHOR

**Immaculée Ilibagiza** is the *New York Times* bestselling author of *Left to Tell, Led by Faith, Our Lady of Kibeho* and *The Boy Who Met Jesus*. She was born in Rwanda and studied electronic and mechanical engineering at the National University. She lost most of her family during the 1994 genocide. Four years later, she emigrated to the United States and soon began working at the United Nations in New York City. She is now a full-time public speaker and writer. In 2007 she established the Left to Tell Charitable Fund, which helps support Rwandan orphans, and was awarded the Mahatma Gandhi International Award for Reconciliation and Peace.

**www.immaculee.com**

# Hay House Titles of Related Interest

*YOU CAN HEAL YOUR LIFE, the movie,*
starring Louise Hay & Friends
(available as an online streaming video)
www.hayhouse.com/louise-movie

*THE SHIFT, the movie,*
starring Dr. Wayne W. Dyer
(available as an online streaming video)
www.hayhouse.com/the-shift-movie

\*\*\*

*EMBRACE YOUR POWER: A Woman's Guide to Loving Yourself, Breaking Rules, and Bringing Good into Your Life,* by Louise Hay

*MIRACLES NOW: 108 Life-Changing Tools for Less Stress, More Flow, and Finding Your True Purpose,* by Gabrielle Bernstein

*THE POWER OF AWAKENING: Mindfulness Practices and Spiritual Tools to Transform Your Life,* by Dr. Wayne W. Dyer

*TRUST YOUR VIBES: Live an Extraordinary Life by Using Your Intuitive Intelligence,* by Sonia Choquette

All of the above are available at www.hayhouse.co.uk

\*\*\*

# Hay House Podcasts
## Bring Fresh, Free Inspiration Each Week!

Hay House proudly offers a selection of life-changing audio content via our most popular podcasts!

### Hay House Meditations Podcast

Features your favorite Hay House authors guiding you through meditations designed to help you relax and rejuvenate. Take their words into your soul and cruise through the week!

### Dr. Wayne W. Dyer Podcast

Discover the timeless wisdom of Dr. Wayne W. Dyer, world-renowned spiritual teacher and affectionately known as "the father of motivation." Each week brings some of the best selections from the 10-year span of Dr. Dyer's talk show on Hay House Radio.

### Hay House Podcast

Enjoy a selection of insightful and inspiring lectures from Hay House Live events, listen to some of the best moments from previous Hay House Radio episodes, and tune in for exclusive interviews and behind-the-scenes audio segments featuring leading experts in the fields of alternative health, self-development, intuitive medicine, success, and more! Get motivated to live your best life possible by subscribing to the free Hay House Podcast.

Listen on
Apple Podcasts

*Find Hay House podcasts on iTunes, or visit www.HayHouse.com/podcasts for more info.*

## CONNECT WITH
# HAY HOUSE
## ONLINE

🌐 hayhouse.co.uk          **f** @hayhouse

📷 @hayhouseuk             🐦 @hayhouseuk

▶ @hayhouseuk             ♪ @hayhouseuk

*Find out all about our latest books & card decks • Be the first to know about exclusive discounts • Interact with our authors in live broadcasts • Celebrate the cycle of the seasons with us • Watch free videos from your favourite authors • Connect with like-minded souls*

'*The gateways to wisdom and knowledge are always open.*'

**Louise Hay**